uubold

Where Money Grows on Trees

An Immigrant's Story of Heartbreak, Resilience, and Triumph

Lupe Christensen

Table of Contents

Dedication

To my fabulous kids and wonderful family.

I love you!

Acknowledgement

To my two children, Sophia and Morty – you are my oxygen. Thank you for the many hours spent helping me with typing, editing, and providing feedback. Your support and encouragement mean the world to me.

To my mom, Lupe Soto, for writing and sharing her journal with me and inspiring me to write this book.

A special thank you to my sister Anabel and brother Chayo for providing invaluable advice and support.

I am deeply grateful for my siblings who provided valuable information about my mom's journey.

Foreword

You may have seen my mother today.

Grandmotherly and wearing plain, neat, quality but old-fashioned clothing, Guadalupe ("Lupe") Soto would have been walking down a sidewalk on her way to visit friends in the modest-size San Joaquin Valley farming town of Lindsay, where she long ago created a secure home for her large family.

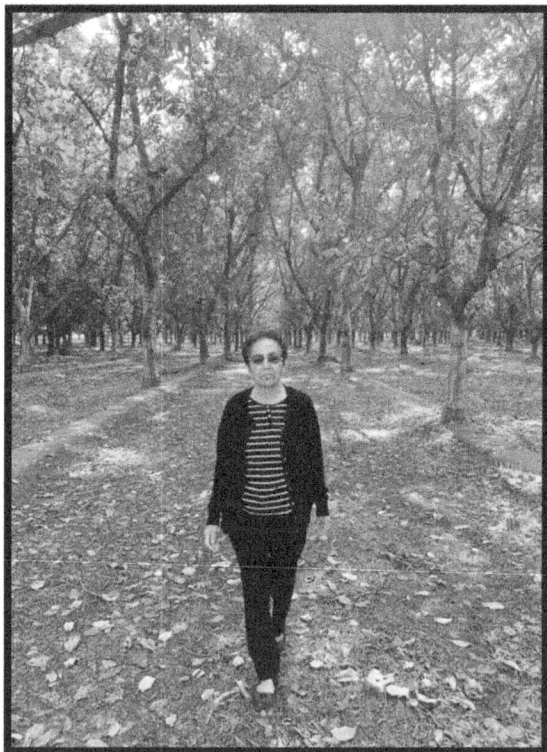

Lupe may have escaped your notice, being just another *abuelita*, an elderly Mexican-American woman.

Widowed, her face was well-lined by time and excessive sun exposure from leading her family as they harvested crops throughout California and the Pacific Northwest, month after month and year after year. But long ago, against tremendous odds, Lupe Soto saved her husband and family from mortal danger and helped their many children establish secure new lives in a new country that both wanted and did not want them.

A stranger herself in this challenging land, Lupe led the way while striving to create a place in a country that offered hard work combined with a path to citizenship and, hopefully, acceptance in this new land.

Older, brown-skinned women like her remain mostly invisible to the world—but not to their adoring families or the Latino community itself, which reveres its elders for the central roles they play in nurturing the life-sustaining weave of their family's legacy.

Lupe Soto's story is filled with incidents that will move anyone with an open heart. It is a personal journey of determination to survive and then thrive against all odds, all for the sake of her family. It proves how the most profound aspects of life are often hidden in plain sight, to be found in the lives of plain-seeming people.

Lupe's story illuminates a Mexican-American family's migrant journey, led by a courageous young mother in her twenties, a woman who initially did not speak the language or understand the culture, norms, or customs of this great country she loves. She forged a permanent home here for herself, Juan Soto—my loving yet tragically flawed father—and their offspring, myself included. *increase line space* →

Our family's story spotlights many seldom-acknowledged sides of Latino culture—its towering work ethic, its fully embraced heritage of devotion to family, and its love of others who show they're willing to be friends and allies. These "foreign influences" have become a vital presence in the United States of America. This nation desperately needs the deep, true warmth Latinos freely extend to anyone willing, in even the slightest way, to be a *compadre.*

My mother, Guadalupe Soto, is the most courageous woman I've ever known. This book is built with love from her truly dramatic life story, as she has patiently recorded and reflected upon it in her old age, using a drugstore notebook and a yellow No. 2 pencil.

To her, the pages she created were just a setting down of events. To me, they are a history *muy rico con vida,* a rich, vivid picture of the courage, determination, and survival instincts she showed, often in desperation, to provide her children futures in which they might thrive—despite an overnight loss of once-considerable status and wealth and the resultant despair and alcoholism that, for all practical purposes, stole her husband away.

It's the journey of a woman-led family struggling for their lives, chased out of their homeland by mortal danger. And so my mother's story is a story for right now, in this time of turmoil and bewilderment regarding immigration, just as much it is an important window into the America where these events took place.

Lupe sometimes shared with us her stories of pain, but only on rare occasions. She had to initially leave her children in Mexico to search the United States for Juan, her errant husband (my father). Then, gathering us up into a migratory life that followed harvest seasons up the length of California and into the orchards of Idaho, Oregon and Washington, she kept us on track, notwithstanding our grievous struggle, to have better lives for ourselves and for the families we six children would one day establish in this new land.

As a little girl hearing bits and pieces of my family's history, I envisioned colorful movies inside my head, inspired by these stories, composed of scenes with captions like the superhero comic books I loved to read. Now I know that the heroism involved, brought forward by a woman who would journey through hell rather than give up on her family, was deeper than my young mind could conceive. And yet, for the rest of her life, she has questioned every painstaking decision she made as a young mother, tormenting herself about the impact her choices might have had on her children.

For her, it has been a lifetime of guilt, doubt, and questioning, but to me, she is a true superhero, a woman who risked everything and gave everything to save the lives of my father, myself, and my siblings, a young Latina mother who spent her life in pursuit of new possibilities for her kids.

My family lived just one out of the millions of tales of immigrants who struggled through malice, discrimination, and poverty and survived, but I believe it is among the deepest and most dramatic examples. And yet it shares much with the stories of all families who have reached America from all over the world, beyond just south of the border.

Our common ground, the ligament that tugs us all together, is that the overwhelming majority of families who migrate to this country simply pursue the opportunity to work hard in pursuit of the American Dream. They are people with the courage to become forerunners, devoting all their spirit and strength to carving a better future somehow, somewhere, in the American social, cultural, and physical landscape.

All of our heartbreaks and struggles are fundamentally the same, whether we are Mexican-American or any of the countless other hybrid identities that perpetually add flavor, texture, and beauty to this incredibly blessed country we all share.

We already believe that America is great, even while some of its native-born citizens may see things differently. We all want the chance to show America that we have brought something strong and worthy in our hearts, some essential and revitalizing ingredients that will enrich the legendary melting pot.

I am one such immigrant. I was named after my mother. I am in love with her brave heart and grateful for the opportunity to introduce you to her story, courage, and life of beautiful, inspiring, determination-driven sacrifice.

In the fall of 2015, I drove some two hundred miles from my Silicon Valley home to visit Lupe at her little house in California's agricultural heartland. We share the same first name, honoring the Virgin of Guadalupe, the patron saint of Mexico, said to have appeared there nearly six hundred years ago. Mexicans revolted against Spanish rule in 1810, inspired by the American Revolution that occurred just thirty-six years earlier. Their battle cry was "Long live our Lady of Guadalupe."

Within our family, I am still often called Lupita, which means "little Lupe." I'm always proud of that.

Lindsay, the town where my siblings and I grew up and where Lupe still lives, sits almost exactly midway between Fresno and Bakersfield in the San Joaquin Valley, California's vast swath of prime agricultural land. Lindsay is now home to some twelve thousand people. Nearly a third of them live in poverty.

Lupe lives in the front house of a pair of plain little homes on a quarter-acre lot of former farmland. An enthusiastic realtor might call it "ranch style." It's a modest box of stucco in an older section of town, not far from Cairn's Corner, a country junction where a produce stand that opened more than a century ago still operates today.

She keeps her home clean and tidy but with an unmistakable vibe of comfort and warmth throughout. Sweet scents of Lupe's cooking greeted me as soon as the front door opened. When I stepped inside, I saw that she had prepared a not-so-small feast. This is what she always does in anticipation of a visit. "Pasate" ("Come in"), she invites as she wraps her retired limbs around me and plants an endless kiss on my cheeks. "¿Comiste?" ("Did you eat?") "Te ves flaca." ("You look skinny.")

Lupe immediately served me a delicious plateful of rice alongside three tacos filled with her tender and juicy carne asada, chile colorado y verde, and Mexican-style cheese with delectable trimmings. Followed by mouth-

8

watering *pan dulce* (sweet bread), I picked from a variety of *conchas, puerquitos, libros, and novias*, a staple in her kitchen. I was not truly hungry, but in her home, you eat whether hungry or not—and you eat all day, as long as your visit lasts. As soon as another guest appears, the dishing-up ritual starts all over again. Leaving my mother's home is very difficult. The laughter and good conversations make you want to stay forever.

After several pleasing bites of her delicious and familiar cooking, I followed Lupe into her bedroom, where she had been cleaning out some old items.

I offered to help.

Pulling out the drawer of her nightstand, I noticed a slender book I'd never seen before. It was a spiral-bound notebook, one that opened from the top. Its cover displayed wide vertical stripes of coffee brown and burgundy beneath softly rendered Japanese flowers, surrounding a picture of a bonsai tree. Much more Zen than Mexicano.

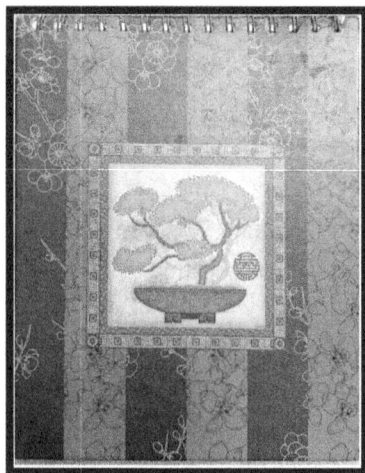

I noticed it was a journal. I thought, "Lupe is journaling? Really?" I gently pulled the journal out of the drawer and asked if I could read a bit.

She assented, telling me in Spanish, "Es algo que vengo escribiendo desde hace un tiempo. Nunca lo he compartido con nadie porque aún no he terminado. Pensé que tal vez después de que me vaya, tú o tu hermana Anabel lo encontrarían." ("It's something that I've been writing for a while now. I've never shared it with anyone because I'm not quite done yet. I thought that maybe after I'm gone, you or your sister, Anabel, would find it.")

I carefully opened her journal to the first page. It was entitled "11-9-05." Lupe had been writing about her life for almost a decade, *en Español*, the language she is still most comfortable in, recording her memories by hand and in pencil. None of her children knew this.

I had read only its first few pages when I began to sob and could not stop. My own life is a blend of Anglo and Mexican, a product of my cultural inheritance, plus my marriage to a man of European descent and my college education and corporate career. I seldom need to use my own Spanish, so even though for many years it was the only language I knew, it now is slightly *limitado*. But Lupe's writing was amazing in its clarity and precision, and her words touched me so deeply, beyond any measure of what I might have expected to feel on seeing her life experiences mounted in a storybook's window.

Lupe had written the full version of many stories that have run like a movie through my head ever since my childhood. Sitting on a corner of a soft bed in my mom's home, I held a collection of her memories. It might contain answers to questions that have puzzled me all my life: Why was Juan, my father, an alcoholic who would eventually drink himself to death? Was my dad's life a slow-motion suicide? Why did Lupe stay with him at all, let alone run off to search for him after he'd disappeared into another country? Where did she gather the strength and energy it took to dedicate her life to the constant uphill battle of keeping all of her family together and alive?

I stopped reading, put a tissue to my eyes, and asked her if we could have a cup of tea together and talk about her journal. It felt like a ceremony as she brewed the tea in her little kitchen. As she poured it into cups, tears ran down and across her beautifully sculpted cheekbones that prove she carries the deepest sort of American roots, the heritage of Indian tribes. Nothing I say or do stops them. Every tear on her face feels like a spear through my heart.

"Yo vivo aquí sola," she began. ("I live here by myself.") "En mi soledad me siento y escribo. Escribo sobre mi vida y pienso en todos los errores que cometí en ella. Me pregunto si hice lo correcto por ti y tus hermanos en las decisiones que tomé como madre. Mis decisiones me persiguen. Pienso en lo diferente que podrían haber sido las cosas si el padre de tu padre hubiera vivido. Tenía tantos planes para la familia." ("In my loneliness I sit and write. I write about my life and think about all the mistakes I made in it. I wonder if I did right by you and your siblings in the decisions I made as a mother. My decisions haunt me. I think how different things could have been if your father's father had lived. He had so many plans for the family.")

11

1. Courtship

Lupe's story began in Michoacán (*Mee-choh-ah-kahn*) de Ocampo, a sprawling west-central Mexican state with rugged mountains and immense tropical beauty, comprising much of the land that separates Guadalajara and Mexico City.

Every year, at the end of summer, some twenty million monarch butterflies fly in from the north to hibernate in the branches of the Michoacán region's plentiful oyamel trees (*Abies religiosa,* or sacred firs). The legs, bodies, and wings of the butterflies are delicate, yet each pilgrim insect has flown nearly a thousand miles to reach Michoacán. After their hibernation is complete, they will need juicy milkweed to sustain themselves. This has to be sought back in northern America. Eventually, the monarchs fly freely across a border that is jealously patrolled to stop humans from crossing.

Lupe will grow up to be a symbolic Michoacán butterfly, *una mariposa humana,* a determined young woman who, in the early 1970s, first legally crossed that border to escape deadly violence and later brought her children across to start brand-new lives in a land where, as Lupe will later tell them, "Money grows on trees. All one has to do is to pick it. And spend it only wisely until it is enough to make your life in this new land better."

Historically, life in those Michoacán mountains is often a struggle. In the sixteenth century, Hérnan Cortés brought forms of pestilence for which indigenous people had no immunity, as well as galleons full of soldiers and rifles that turned natives into slave laborers mining gold for the *conquistadores.* In 1910, the Mexican Revolution inspired landless peasants by the thousands to fight for liberation from elites who held them in servitude in a share-cropping system much like the one that kept freed African Americans a good deal less than free. Attacks by insurgent mobs, wide-open banditry, drought, and epidemics ravaged Michoacán and most other parts of Mexico. Political fortunes shifted again and again, a bruising dance between counter-revolutionaries and revolutionaries, in which hundreds of thousands fled Mexico and an estimated 1.5 million people—roughly 10 percent of the nation's population—lost their lives.

Our story starts in Michoacán in 1928.

A beautiful, fair-skinned, athletic fourteen-year-old girl named Trina blossomed early into an outstanding beauty. She was taller than most girls and not at all fond of school. For this early twentieth-century time and this old-fashioned, strict, and tradition-bound part of Mexico, Trina

13

was a very free-spirited teenage girl, full of life and outgoing. Though very smart, she ditched school frequently. Trina and her best friend, Xiomara, walked to school on a dirt path every morning, along with other schoolmates. While the other kids arrived at their classroom, Trina and Xiomara snuck away before coming within sight of the schoolhouse, edging off their path to arrive at a riverbank.

A tall, beautiful tree sat perfectly in its place along the river, not far from a small, two-story house that belonged to the Soto family, which owned quite a lot of farmland and cattle. They were the most important family for many miles.

The tree had generous shade to protect the girls from the hot sun, and its leafy branches were supported by strong limbs. One day, Trina and Xiomara tied a rope on a stout tree limb and took turns swinging out over the river.

Trina at first held onto the rope while her friend climbed. Trina pushed Xiomara back and forth. Very soon, she gathered a nice momentum and swung far enough over the river to let go of the rope and make a satisfying splash into the river. The girls had never heard of such a thing as an amusement park, but if such a thing existed, this rope over the river would have been everyone's favorite ride.

Trina went next. She put her well-worn shoes safely by the trunk of the tree. Her heart pumped quickly with excitement as she climbed out on the limb to grab the rope. Just as her girlfriend did, she pushed off and swung back and forth on the rope until her momentum launched her into the warm, silky waters of the inviting river.

Both girls spent their time laughing, butterflying, and backstroking. Their classmates spent their day at school. Xiomara and Trina joined them later, just in time for the end-of-day bell. Then, they walked back home alongside the other kids. Their teacher and the girls had an understanding: if they kept up with their studies and helped her clean the chalkboards and dust erasers, their secret was safe with her. And so, Trina and Xiomara kept their promise to stay after school to help the teacher clean.

One morning, Trina began her usual dirt-path walk to school. Two men suddenly appeared on horseback. One of them lunged his horse up alongside Trina. Rotating himself in the saddle, he wrapped a powerful arm around her waist, lifted her off the ground, and then wrangled her onto the back of his horse. She must have held on for dear life as the two horses and three riders galloped away from the village toward the craggy hills surrounding it. Trina screamed and punched as much as a fourteen-year-old girl could. She knew the men worked for the Soto family and demanded an explanation. The men carried on without a word. Finally stopping at a remote cabin, they delivered the abducted girl to a kindly older woman who lived there. As soon as they rode off, the woman explained to the teenage girl what had just happened.

Her kidnappers worked for Don Rosario Soto, the wealthiest *ranchero* in the land, and had fetched her to the cabin because he desired Trina in marriage. Rosario Soto was *comisario* (deputy) of this portion of Michoacán. With such power, he stood, for the most part, as the arbiter of right and wrong in his territory.

15

But even though she was stolen from the village, Trina had a choice in the matter. Her abduction was an assertion of alpha male privilege, although, in rural Mexico in 1928, such high-handedness was within normal bounds, at least for the most important men. Many would say that it carries a chivalrous veneer. Rosario remained at a distant location, awaiting her decision.

Rosario was a rich man with a kind heart, a trait that solidified his respect among local people. He was seen as strong yet fair and often called upon to settle local disputes. He also loaned money, operated stores, and owned land and cattle. Rosario often excused the poorer local people from their debts to him. If he knew they were in need, he added free groceries to their orders.

In short, Rosario Soto was an aristocrat. If he sought a beautiful young wife and resorted to courtship by abduction, such privileged behavior was his due (at least in rural Mexico of nearly a century ago).

Trina was in a predicament. If she rejected him, the community would judge her to be dishonored, and her virginity would be assumed to have been taken. If she accepted him, she'd be wed to a man many years senior to her. And in fact, she found Rosario handsome, powerful, and charismatic. Nevertheless, days passed at the hideaway cabin before she acceded.

By ultimately saying yes, she was soon blessed with a life of servants and queenly indulgence. Rosario's home was a true hacienda, a grand dwelling with many lesser structures surrounding it, in a setting *muy rico con vida*, rich in life and natural beauty. Two maids were devoted to

16

serving Trina. A *maestro*, a teacher, was hired to read her books and handle whatever correspondence was required to run the household's affairs.

There were many more workers, including gardeners and cooks, to ensure that Rosario's young bride was treated like a treasure. He remained smitten with Trina for the rest of his life.

The marriage was eventually blessed with a son named Juan. He would grow into a handsome and much-admired young man, six feet tall, intent on learning the intricacies of his father's dealings and holdings so that he could become an excellent steward of the family's business in the future. All of the Soto empire would be his one day.

Because this fine fortune was paired with a proud masculine bearing, Juan Soto was known to be the grandest catch, the "golden boy," of this part of Michoacán.

2. La Vuelta

Guadalupe Lorenzo came into this world in 1940 in Santa Fe del Rio, a community not far from the Soto domain. She completed fifth grade in a Catholic school for girls. Her father, a tailor, prohibited further education. His decision was yet another assertion of alpha male privilege. For Lupe, a sixth-grade education would have to take place in a nonsectarian, co-ed setting. Her father would not allow his daughter to be in danger of having her virtue compromised by rumors that she appeared interested in boys. Lupe wanted to continue with her education; however, there was no other option but to quit school.

However, by the time Lupe was in her teens, both her father and mother allowed her to join in the fiesta tradition called *paseo*. The fifteenth of August was *el dia de la Asuncion de Maria* (the Day of the Assumption of Mary), a religious feast celebrating the Virgin Mary's arrival in Heaven and celebrated in Catholic churches worldwide, including Mexico. The town's plaza, the setting for a fair with games and rides, was alive with celebration.

During the Santa Fe del Rio Fiesta, groups of girls who were accompanied by chaperones could spend a part of the evening's celebration ambling as a group in a big circle around the town plaza.

Boys simultaneously circulated in the opposite direction, able to openly glimpse (with respectful discretion) the marriageable girls from whom they may select a young local beauty as a focus for their attention. This ceremony was the approved way of finding love in Mexican tradition. Every moment and every movement was under the scrutiny of older women who simply did not smile while on duty.

In this *vuelta*, Juan Soto saw Guadalupe Lorenzo walking along with her three best friends, Raquel Espinosa, Eva Romero, and Lupe Jacobo. They walked their circular route locked shoulder to shoulder, as if presenting themselves and defending themselves in the same gesture. They all noticed Juan Soto. In fact, the other three girls feasted their eyes on him as if he were a celebrity.

Juan walked the Paseo with some of his amigos. Lupe knew of him, just as all the local girls did, but she did not fancy him. He was just a *habitante del campo*, a country boy. She was a native of Santa Fe del Rio, itself part of the

19

municipality Penjamillo de Degollado, a place of beauty and history that Viceroy Carlos de Medici, a scion of the powerful Florentine family, founded some four centuries ago. So, Lupe was proud and choosy, and her beauty permitted her that indulgence. Her previous suitor, Sebastian, was a doctor. But he was also ten years her senior, and eventually, she rejected him.

Lupe had seen Juan around town before, and on different occasions, he'd come somewhat near her. On the night of the fiesta, he looked particularly handsome, wearing a light blue button-up shirt, sharply creased khaki pants, and brown leather shoes of fine quality. His wavy hair was nicely combed back.

The moment came. His eyes locked with Lupe's.

As was the custom, he then approached her with an impressively enormous bouquet of roses. As chaperones

20

watched, the two began calmly talking. They agreed he would pass by her house later with his buddies, but of course would not stop. This tiny flirtation would be their only contact for half a year. Juan had been scheduled to spend the next six months in Monterrey, some 400 miles to the northeast and barely 150 miles away from the Texas border. He would train there as a military police officer.

These months were difficult. Juan missed Lupe, and she missed him. She began to think she must learn to forget the striking boy who gave her roses. But when the news came that Juan had returned from Monterrey, Lupe realized that the news made her feel happy inside. Very soon, it was well-known that they were sweethearts.

As a couple-to-be, Juan and Lupe had to observe strict protocol. He went to visit her at her parents' home but had to remain outside their dwelling. There was absolutely no handholding, kissing, or any other touching. She stayed inside the house, conversing with Juan through an open window.

After a year had passed and decorum had been served, Juan was beyond eager to advance the relationship. He told Lupe of a plan in which they would elope. Lupe insisted instead that Juan ask her father for her hand in marriage in the proper manner. In a show of great formality, Juan sent a priest to the Lorenzo household as his emissary.

The priest arrived at the Lorenzo residence to be greeted by Lupe's Mother, Amelia. She was expecting him. She had prepared a grand feast for the festive occasion in honor of his visit. There was a knock at the door. "Buenas tardes, pase Padre." ("good evening, come in Father.") She said as she opened the door, allowing the thin man to walk through the heavy wooden door. The priest took off his old hat and handed it to Amelia. She led him to the living room, where the rest of the family joined. After a brief conversation, they made their way into the dining room. Amelia served dinner. "Haré que esta visita sea corta y dulce. Juan Soto y su familia me han dado el privilegio de invitarme a visitar su hermosa casa en su nombre. Ellos buscan la mano de Lupe en matrimonio con Juan. Ellos están pidiendo sus bendiciones." The priest stated. ("I will make this visit short and sweet. Juan Soto and his family have given me the privilege of asking me to come visit your lovely home on their behalf. They are seeking Lupe's hand in marriage to Juan. They are asking for your blessings.") When the priest respectfully asked on Juan's behalf for her hand in marriage, Lupe's parents were ecstatic. Lupe's parents assured the priest that Juan and Lupe had their blessings. Lupe wanted to wed Juan in a year. He wanted to be married right away. She countered with marriage six months from the day she accepted his proposal and asserted that she may need a month or two to decide. Juan said no, the wedding itself must happen in two months.

Lupe wanted them to each be sure of their choice. Ultimately, the marriage would be a full year away, and Juan had to endure as patiently as possible. Soon, Juan's parents, Trina and Rosario, began visiting Lupe's parents to get to know each other and start preparation for the wedding. Rosario gave Lupe money every time he visited to buy whatever she needed for the wedding. His generosity helped Lupe understand why Juan sometimes seemed like a spoiled child.

Lupe was as excited to wed Juan as any bride could be. To shop for her wedding dress, she traveled to a wonderful bridal boutique in La Piedad, the largest nearby municipality, with her sister Teresa and two close friends. Trina, her future mother-in-law, was also there for support. Lupe decided on an all-white, princess-style dress, a very fashionable choice, combining it with a beautiful crown and veil. Trina then revealed that Juan had sent money with her to pay for whichever dress and accessories Lupe desired. This filled her with warmth and joy. She now knew that she made the right choice for her life partner.

Their wedding finally arrived, lasting four days of celebration. The golden boy had given his heart, an event of great local significance. Families throughout the region sent pigs, turkeys, chickens, goats, and sheep as gifts meant to provision the feast, befitting the Soto family's stature.

The ceremony was in a Santa Fe del Rio church, beautifully dressed in flowing white curtains. Tall white flowers adorned each pew to create a fairy-tale atmosphere. Dignitaries, government officials, and uniformed soldiers filled the church, along with numerous friends and family.

The most honored guests convened at Rosario and Trina's hacienda after the wedding. Lupe and Juan arrived and began dancing. Through nearly two years of courtship, they have never danced together, because that would have brought scandal. Finally, in one another's arms, they danced as though they never wanted to stop. Tables were arrayed on the patio in white linen, radiating outward from the flowing fountain in the center of the hacienda's garden. Lupe's wedding day seemed to fly by. It was ten at night when she ceremoniously threw her bridal bouquet away. But in lieu of a honeymoon night with her young groom, Lupe went separately to the home of her godparents. This reflected a strong Catholic belief that a new bride should spend four days and nights apart from her husband. In the wedding ceremony, she had received Christ via the Eucharist ceremony. It was deemed proper, the priest instructed Lupe, to wait a respectable amount of time before sharing herself with a man.

When her godparents delivered Lupe to the Soto home, the hacienda was still full of people celebrating. Their celebration would continue for three more days.

3. Rosario

Lupe and Juan set up their household at the Soto hacienda, and before long, they added to the family's considerable treasures. Alberto was their firstborn. Both Rosario and Juan were ecstatic that the first child was a boy.

One year later came Rosario, named for his grandfather. Both boys were treated as special. Lupe dressed them in high-quality clothing, with nice leather shoes and proper hats to shield the youngsters from Mexico's hot sun. Two years later, the family was blessed with a beautiful baby girl, Anabel. With lovely features that mirrored Trina's beauty, she became their little princess.

Primitivo came next, a handsome kid with a slender nose, big eyes, and full lashes just like Lupe's. Then another baby girl arrived. When Lupe was pregnant with her, Juan was away on business in the United States. He wanted to be at home for the birth but could not make it back in time.

Lupe wanted to name their new girl something precious, like Rubi (Ruby) or perhaps Perla (Pearl). Juan said he had a better idea and would reveal it when he came back home. She was holding her unnamed second daughter in her arms when Juan arrived to say, "Lupita. Como tu." "Lupita. Just like you."

Lupita, of course, means "little Lupe." Juan's choice made Lupe's heart beat faster, just like the day he surprised her by paying for her wedding dress.

With the couple's sixth baby, Juanito, it was Juan who acquired a namesake. Juanito was by far the cutest baby. Trina, in particular, adored him and made sure he was well taken care of, well-dressed, and professionally photographed at every opportunity. He had the perfect nose, beautiful sleepy brown eyes, and a beautiful smile that melted everyone's heart. He grew into a quiet yet very observant and smart little boy, loved by everyone.

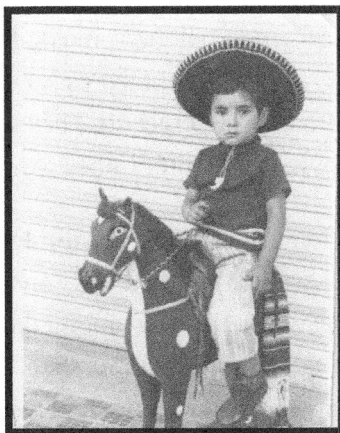

Lupe watched her children grow up in a happy home, showered with lots of attention and love. When their grandfather Rosario was not holding as many of his six grandchildren as possible in his lap, he was busy planning their futures. He prepaid medical school tuition for Alberto. All the grandkids were to attend private colleges in Spain. Lupe was glad that her father-in-law took such practical interest, but her greatest happiness lay in watching her children run and jump up into their Grandfather Soto's lap.

Lupe cared little about luxury, though an easy life could be hers for the asking. Her focus was on her little family's well-being and its wholesome lifestyle. To this end, she participated in many of the enterprises that brought income to her in-laws. Like Juan, she foresaw that she would eventually have to assume greater responsibilities, so she wished to be ready for that moment.

Rosario loved entertaining and enjoyed having people over for dinner and drinks. One of the kids' favorite activities was watching movies after nightfall in the backyard. Rosario loaded a movie projector, tacked up a bedsheet on an exterior wall, and showed knockabout comedies featuring the great Cantinflas or guitar-slinger vaquero music fests starring Tito Guizar. *Comedias rancheras,* comedies set on a ranch or in a small town, were frequently screened. The ladies also admired Elvis Presley's movies, including Lupe.

Guests often joined the family for these magical evenings: politicians, nearby families, and other everyday people of Michoacán. These were among the years historians called the golden age of Mexican cinema, as the country's film industry began gaining international respect.

Rosario loved seeing his family and all the other visiting people share these moments, not least because of his pride in being the popular and prosperous man who could provide them. Rosario was a handsome man, flourishing in late middle age, who was giving, kind, and trusting. He was tall, with dark, wavy hair and fair skin, loving each grandchild nearly as much as he revered his Trina.

Among other businesses, the Sotos ran a farm supply store, a grocery store, a liquor store, a dairy, a corn mill, a deli selling fresh fruit and *licuados* (fresh-fruit-based drinks), plus a meat market, and a bakery that provided fresh bread daily. He also owned many heads of cattle, numerous horses, and several acres of land—much of it used for cultivating the crops that supplied his stores.

Like many Mexicans of this post–Great Depression era, Rosario didn't trust banks. His voluminous income was often stuffed into suitcases that were simply kept in closets or under beds at home. Money also got buried and sealed within the stucco walls of the family's hacienda, under a fresh coat of plaster.

Juan busied himself with cattle, ranching, and harvesting the land. At the end of a long day, he and his *compañeros* gathered for abundant drinks. It's a predilection that would remain with him for years to come.

4. Murder in Michoacán

On the night of February 14, 1970, everything changed. It was Valentine's Day, which people in Mexico have always celebrated as the day of love and friendship. Rosario was lying down on a chaise outside, and Juan was with him. Lupe could faintly hear them chatting in the distance. She and her sister-in-law, Angelina Soto, went to bed. Raquel, Trina's adopted daughter, had gone to bed earlier. Trina's sister passed while giving birth to Raquel. Trina adopted Raquel, and her two older siblings went to live with another aunt. They were sound asleep when someone came up to knock on her door. It was Jose, a nephew of Rosario's. His voice was strained and difficult to hear. He did not set foot inside. Lupe found him trying to sit up on a round stone outside next to the door. By the time she reached him, Trina had also awakened and came out to see what was happening.

Jose's right hand was carefully cupped against his belly. He had a fresh bullet wound. A disturbing swath of blood was spreading across the white cloth of his shirt. Jose could not bear the pain and could not walk without help. He asked Lupe and Trina to support him in struggling to reach his own house.

Trina grabbed him by one arm, and Lupe took the other. As they dragged Jose down the street, his legs were barely able to help them advance. He cringed and begged them to let him stop and rest upon a log that served as a rustic bench laid on its side and flattened on top to provide a sitting place outside a neighbor's front door.

Jose could no longer stand the pain of trying to move. His groans awakened the woman who lived in that house. Her name was Amelia, and she was Rosario's cousin. She and Rosario, who had also responded to Jose's cries of pain, went to fetch his family.

In a very short time, Jose's entire family came to provide help and comfort. Jose was overmatched by the intensity of his pain. He asked his family to drive him to the city to see a doctor because the doctors in this small ranching community were not well qualified or experienced, and his life was in the balance.

The family asked Lupe to go get Juan, who was still back at the house asleep. She woke him up. And as she and Juan arrived at Amelia's, two ranch workers also showed up. Pepe and Jorge drove a station wagon that belonged to Jose. They managed to lay him on blankets in the cargo area as Juan immediately jumped into the driver's seat. He, Pepe, and Jorge drove off out of town so rapidly that Lupe had no chance to ask where they were taking the wounded man. Everything just happened too fast.

When Juan was out traveling, Angelina would usually stay over and sleep with Lupe in her bedroom. The two of them laid back down to sleep. Later, at a time that Lupe could not recall, she heard knocking on the door. It was very late at night, and yet other people could be heard talking on the street.

Raquel, Trina's adopted daughter whom they took in after her mother died at birth, was fast asleep in her bedroom.

Lupe turned in her bed and went back to sleep, not alarmed by the knocking. The Soto family owned several stores, one of them even located right next door. It often happened that Rosario got up to sell things to people who were in emergency situations. In Lupe's sleepy mind, nothing strange or out of the ordinary was happening. Then she had a curious thought, a sense of disturbance, but immediately ignored it and did not let it command her attention. Angelina remained fast asleep, as they both had to get up early the next day. Lupe fluffed up her pillow and kept sleeping.

At dawn, she called on Angelina to get up and accompany her. This was a day when they had to make menudo to sell in the store. Both women climbed out of bed, dressed, and headed to the kitchen. Then they heard a knock on the door and went to open it.

Socorro, their neighbor, appeared to be trying to hold back tears. She screamed, "¡Pronto! ¡Dense prisa, Angelina y Lupe! (Hurry, Angelina and Lupe! Hurry!) "Rosario está tirado en la calle, frente a la casa de Cruz Espinosa, iba camino al molino y lo vi allí, en el suelo." ("Rosario is lying in the street, across from Cruz Espinosa's house! I was on my way to the mill, and I saw him there, on the ground.")

Both women were in shock. For several moments, they could not move or speak as they looked at each other in disbelief. They each did the sign of the cross, Lupe reciting, "Ay Dios mio, en el nombre del Padre y del Hijo y del Espíritu Santo, amen" ("In the name of the Father and of the Son and of the Holy Spirit, amen.") as they struggled to fully comprehend what Socorro said.

Then they rushed out the kitchen door. Lupe felt scared and confused, and her heart began pounding so loudly that she could feel it beating heavily.

On the street, they at first saw no one. The sunrise was breaking lightly through the sky. Typically, during this time of day, people would be hustling about, going off to work at first light as is commonplace in the countryside. But on this day, no one wanted to come out of their homes. They were afraid for their own lives.

And then they saw Rosario supine in the street. The blood pooled beneath him seemed as big as a fish pond. Lupe fell to her knees next to him. She grabbed his chest and shook him. "¡Rosario, despierta por favor!" she demanded. ("Wake up, please!") He was unresponsive. She desperately placed her hand on his wounds to stop the bleeding but soon realized it was too late. Rosario was dead.

Angelina fell to his side, pressing her head on his chest and begging for him to wake. In shock, she refused to get up or move or leave his side. Her father, practically a king within this Michoacán domain, has just bled out his life on a dirty street. Lupe got up, ran to a nearby neighbor who barely cracked open the door, and asked for a blanket to cover his body. As she ran back, in her mind, she hoped this was all a nightmare.

Rosario had been taken at gunpoint from his home in the middle of the night. That was the sound Lupe had dreamily heard. Gunmen working for the powerful Espinosa family (a pseudonym for reasons of present-day safety) carried out Rosario's murder. Jose had killed David Melos, an Espinosa nephew, in the gunfire exchange in which he had been so grievously wounded. The Espinosas forced themselves into Rosario's home. The Soto patriarch had asked that they not kill him in his own home, for his family's sake. They considered his request, then the three men took him out of his home at gunpoint to be executed in the street. The three men dragged Rosario through the streets all the way near their territory across from an intersection. They began to fire, 69 bullets destroyed Rosario's body.

Rosario had been rich and yet a humble, warmhearted, and charismatic man. His greatest pleasure seemed to have been in hosting and entertaining—not only his own children and grandchildren but also distant relatives and local friends who frequently came to enjoy his great hospitality. And now he was dead. Juan, meanwhile, was out of town somewhere. Lupe had no clue how to reach him or where or to whom she might turn.

The Mexican custom is to bury the dead within one day of their passing. In fulfilling her duty to prepare Rosario for a final viewing, Trina fainted repeatedly. Lupe soldiered on, preparing Rosario for his wake, hoping vainly that her own husband would be able to see his murdered father one last time.

The news of Rosario's demise traveled fast. Later that same morning, family arrived from a nearby ranch, followed by friends and Lupe's mother and father, who arrived from their Santa Fe del Rio home.

Despite the large number of friends and family Rosario had and his great importance and influence within the community, few other people showed up. It was strange to see just a handful of men, barely enough to be counted on the fingers of one hand. When they laid Rosario out in the house, Trina again passed out repeatedly, and the women of the family could not stabilize her fainting spells.

Later, three of Juan's half-sisters arrived in a taxi from La Piedad de Cabadas, the nearest city, with news of Juan. He had taken Jose to La Piedad for doctoring.

The family members all agreed that the best thing was for Lupe to give Juan the news in person. No one could predict how he might react. At the very least, his wife would be there to accompany him in his moment of extreme pain. Then, she could bring Juan back to the Ranch.

Not knowing how Juan would react when learning of his father's death, Lupe boarded the taxi back to La Piedad to search for her husband.

As she climbed into the taxi, Lupe's mother said, "voy con mi hija. No dejaré que Lupe se vaya sola. Es demasiado peligroso para una mujer viajar sola después de una experiencia tan traumática y con un peligro tan persistente." ("I'm going with my daughter. I will not let Lupe go alone. It is just too dangerous for a woman to be traveling alone after such a traumatic experience and with such lingering danger.")

Then Izzy, one of Rosario's sons-in-law, also joined them as protection.

Piedad means "mercy" in Spanish. Lupe had never before felt so in need of such a blessing.

5. Searching for Juan

Upon arrival in La Piedad, Lupe and her mother searched hospitals, clinics, medical centers, and private doctors' offices. They could not find either Juan or Jose. So next, they supposed that the men had probably gone to Irapuato, a larger city that was also nearby.

They did not find the men in Irapuato either. Lupe felt like she could not deal with the situation any longer. She was overwhelmed by many emotions, fears, and anxieties. She loved Rosario as if he had been her own father. His death hurt her so much, and she could barely guess how greatly his death would impact their lives.

The women returned as they had left—tired, empty handed and with such great regret and heartache. They arrived just in time for Rosario's funeral. The patriarch was buried in a very simple fashion. Some family and most of his friends, were afraid to be seen honoring someone whose enemies were so bloodthirsty. Lupe's sister Esperanza (Cuca) took care of the children. They were very small and did not understand what was going on. Their mother did not want to expose them to such a devastating situation, and she could not attend to them and her mother-in-law.

Juanito was the youngest at that time, a month away from turning one year old. The oldest was Alberto, not quite ten. Lupe had six kids to care for. She was twenty-nine years old and alone with such huge problems. She could not think clearly. She felt alone, desperate that she did not know the whereabouts of her husband. She had to somehow reach him

35

and share the terrible news of his dad. She wanted Juan to know so that he could see his father one last time before they buried him. It was all extremely sad, and in the same instant, she was concerned for the safety of her children and her husband.

Two days later, news arrived: Jose was recuperating in Michoacán's capital city, about seventy miles to the south. Juan, Pepe, and Jorge were locked in a Morelia jail cell. The Espinosas had accused them of aiding Jose in the murder.

It was another shock for Lupe, who was already overwhelmed by the fact that her father-in-law had been executed and all the underpinnings of her own family had been ripped out. Not only was the patriarch of her family gone, but her innocent husband was imprisoned, her mother-in-law was sick, and her six small children needed her more than ever. She felt like the world was caving in and her life was over. How could she ever again be happy?

Many such thoughts passed through her head. Throughout her entire life, she'd had the full support of her family. Rosario had been her mentor and her security. Now, he was gone. Who could she turn to for comfort or direction?

Lupe made plans to visit Juan, but shortly before she could set off to Morelia, she got a message from him, relayed with the help of a relative. She was not to worry, but she should not go to see him in jail. His case had been closed. He and the other two men could prove they had been home when David Melos was killed. Juan wanted Lupe to stay away safely with the children. For the time being, the Federales believed he was safer in jail than out. Rather than release him in Morelia, the police intended to transport all three men to La Piedad. Their lives were in danger.

Men carrying guns hired by the Espinosas were guarding the entrances to the Ranch and other ranches nearby, with orders to kill Juan, Pepe, and Jorge if they returned to the Ranch. The police needed time for the situation to diffuse enough for them to take back control of the area. Juan had previously served in the Servicio Militar Nacional (National Military Service), so he was well-connected politically and could count on some police help.

Soon, the three men arrived in La Piedad under police escort. Juan then sent another message to Lupe: "Vente a La Piedad y traite al niño chiquito nada más y traite la pistola." ("Come to La Piedad with our little baby, Juanito, and carry a gun.")

Lupe was to travel with Enrique, a ranch worker who was also Juan's most trusted confidant. He helped her escape to La Piedad, about one hour away, where Juan was staying in the home of a woman named Laura.

Laura was the mother of three daughters whom Rosario had fathered out of wedlock. She and the children were supported by Rosario, and Juan bet his life that the Espinosas did not know of this almost family relationship. Lupe and Juan stayed at Laura's for a few days, deciding how to shape their futures as safely as possible. They both agreed not to return to the Ranch.

Juan wrote a letter to his mother, Trina, telling her of a plan to make a home in La Piedad, then pick up the other children. Soon, Trina, Raquel, and Angelina arrived with a truck loaded to capacity with beds and almost all of Juan and Lupe's household items. Trina and Angelina had also decided to leave the Ranch. They did not want there to be a reason for Juan to return and give the men an opportunity to kill him. Or for him to have an opportunity to kill them in retribution. A rented house in La Piedad would be everyone's home for the time being.

The biggest problem remaining was that Juan, who had always loved to drink, now drank heavily. Since his father's death, he got deeply intoxicated every day.

Even though the family began to feel safer in La Piedad, this was an ugly and dangerous time. Juan drank with a gun at his side. He did not know whom he could trust and struggled with fear and anger every waking moment. He did not know how to mourn the starkly brutal death of his father and the loss of his own young family's once-secure future. He wrestled with his powerlessness, guilt, and sadness and descended into undeniable alcoholism. Rosario's wisdom and wealth had always provided whatever Juan needed. Without them, he did not know what to do next.

Juan became fixated on avenging Rosario's death. He became an angry and bitter man. The sweet, loving, and caring man Lupe once married and with whom she had her children disappeared. Juan walked around with a rifle in hand and made Lupe carry a gun, too. There was one road into and out of La Piedad in the direction of the Ranch. Juan patrolled the entrance to the city, looking for people coming from the Ranch. He stopped passenger trucks and buses in search of the enemy.

Eventually, Juan convinced Lupe to return with him to the Ranch. They spent an anxious day there asking questions, looking for the men behind Rosario's murder.

Late in the day, when they attempted to leave, twelve men with rifles and guns surrounded their truck. Juan reached for the door handle and, at the same moment, grabbed the gun lying on the seat next to him. Seeing this, Lupe began to pray out loud. But before the violence that seemed inevitable could unfold, a powerful voice outside the truck said, "Leave them alone! Let them go. We have a long line of cars holding back traffic."

This was the last time Lupe and Juan ever saw the ancestral lands that Rosario had always meant to entrust to them.

6. New Beginnings

Every day was the same. Juan could not accept the death of his father. He cried, shouted, blasphemed, and did not understand reason. Any mention of the Ranch ignited something within him, and at that moment, he hated everyone, including Lupe and the rest of his family. He combined them in his mind with everything that made him furious.

They were all afraid of this transformed man, and everyone hid from him as much as possible.

There in La Piedad, Trina and Lupe could not think of what to do with Juan. Finally, they took him to a doctor, who insisted that Juan had to stop drinking. Juan wanted to stop but could not do so on his own.

Along with lots of advice, the doctor prescribed a drug to help him quit alcohol. The role of this medicine was to cause unpleasant effects if Juan consumed even small amounts of alcohol, such as headache, nausea, blurred vision, mental confusion, breathing difficulty, and anxiety. However, if the dosage was too small, the drug would do no good, and if too large, it could cause psychotic reactions. And then there was the terrible stress that drove Juan to drink excessively in the first place. He had been the golden boy, heir to a great fortune, father to his own brood of precious children who relied on him just as he had relied on his father. Without having alcohol to subdue his many demons, they came back to Juan as harrowing as ever before. So, the medicine was discarded.

Eventually, Juan convinced Lupe of a plan to buy a butcher shop in La Piedad, one that was for sale for three thousand pesos, roughly equivalent to $30,000 American dollars today. And so, the couple went to work. The money was good, and all went well in the butchery, but Juan continued to drink. On the one hand, the business served Lupe as therapy. She was kept too busy to dwell on her problems. But those problems did not disappear. Juan's active alcoholism made him unreliable, so Lupe was really the only one who was working.

Everything in La Piedad seemed so expensive. The family even had to pay for water. It was so different for them than when they were living on the Ranch. Everything they could want was within reach there, and most often, it was given to them for the asking, through Rosario's generosity.

Lupe thanked God every day for not allowing anything bad to happen to her husband on that final day at the Ranch. Their children all needed him to pull through his despondency and his daily alcohol poisoning.

One day, it occurred to Trina that Juan should travel to the United States to get full treatment for his alcoholism. The whole family, even Juan, knew that he was deeply lost in his alcoholic lifestyle and needed saving. Allowing him to continue in this state would surely kill him.

When Juan went to the United States, Lupe had to close down the meat market so she could focus on taking care of their children. Juan said that once he got settled in the United States, he would find a job and send the family money.

But very soon, Lupe realized that their savings were almost gone. It made her nervous not to work, and months went by with no word from Juan, not even a note, much less any money for the family. After a while, Trina and Angelina risked going back to the Ranch to sell some belongings that remained there, like horses and mules, donkeys, oxen, and tools for working the lands. There was also a house that Juan had been given by his grandpa.

Raquel was the only one who stayed with Lupe and her children in La Piedad. No one visited except Lupe's parents and her sister Esperanza. They would sometimes help pay the rent and buy enough groceries for a week. The oldest boys, Alberto and Chayo, were nine and eight years old, respectively. They realized how difficult times were for the family and, on their own, went out to find work. Their part-time work brought in enough money to buy food. Raquel and Lupe did the cooking and cleaning and took care of the four younger children.

Many people in La Piedad knew Lupe because of the meat market. They would always ask her, "What happened with Juan? Does he send you money?"

She would always tell them, yes, but it was not true. She did not want people to know that sometimes her family did not have enough money to eat. These were bitter and sad times because those were the circumstances of her children's lives. She didn't dream he would fail his family, but the weeks and months went by without the reassurance she craved.

In life, one goes through highs and lows, but this was different from the ups and downs of life. Lupe hit bottom.

Raquel helped a bit with buying food or whatever else was needed in the house. When Lupe lived at the Ranch, she and Raquel had taken fashion and sewing classes, so they decided to give classes to girls in their neighborhood. They charged each girl one peso per day, which helped with groceries. But the children were in school, so they needed uniforms, shoes, and money for their lunch and soda at recess time. Those expenses consumed the little bit the two young women were making.

Raquel suffered in conjunction with the family. She never left Lupe alone, nor her children, and she defended the little ones from bullies. She stood by the family through the most difficult moments in La Piedad.

More than half a year passed without any word from Juan. Lupe hoped he was safe and in the United States but knew nothing of his whereabouts or his circumstances.

She went around in circles, restless and worried, trying to decide on the best thing for her to do. Finally, she realized that she needed to look for Juan in the United States. It seemed impossible for her children to grow up without him. They needed their father as soon as possible. They were growing up fast. She needed to find him and for everyone to come together again as a family before it was too late.

Lupe had never traveled away from the corner of Michoacán where she had been born. She thought the United States was perhaps the same distance away as La Piedad was from Mexico City or that a trip there might be like going to Guadalajara. But of course, it was not like that at all. Lupe had no idea what she was getting herself into.

43

Lupe asked Trina and Angelina to return to La Piedad. When they arrived, she told them that she would look for Juan in the United States and wanted Trina to accompany her to Mexico City to arrange for a passport. Then Lupe sent word of her decision to her papá and mamá. They quickly arrived in La Piedad and told their daughter that if she had already made up her mind, God willing, maybe she could succeed.

Lupe had no money at all, but very fortunately, she found someone willing to buy the butcher shop she and Juan had bought. It was the same person who had sold it to them. He gave Lupe three thousand pesos, exactly what she had paid for it.

Then Trina and Lupe were off to Mexico City to arrange for a passport.

7. With Money You Do Not Suffer

When Rosario Soto was still alive, and Lupe and Juan still lived at the Ranch, she had corresponded by mail with her older sister, Teresa.

Teresa and her husband and children had moved a few years earlier to Salinas, a medium-sized California city. There, she and her family owned several grocery stores by the name of El Charito, which is a term of endearment in Spanish. Teresa knew that Lupe was curious about the United States and offered her home if Lupe ever wanted to visit. While living at the Ranch, Lupe sent her a big yes, saying that she had that desire.

Teresa then sent Lupe a letter of support, indicating to the necessary government officials that Lupe could stay with her in the USA. She instructed Lupe that with her letter in hand, she could go to Mexico City to get a permit to cross the border. A letter of support is a document in which someone who is already in the country verifies for the immigration authorities that you are a person of good character and financial standing.

Lupe had kept Teresa's letter for a rainy day and never told a soul about it. She had held onto it through all the terrible things that had happened, and when she thought about going to look for Juan, she remembered that it might help her. She took it to Mexico City, the only documentation she had to start her journey to the United States. She did not know what other documents she might need.

When Lupe and Trina arrived in Mexico City, they headed to the house of Maria, an older cousin who was also Lupe's confirmation godmother.

She said, "Mira hija, no vas a ir sola a buscar a Juan. En primer lugar, eres muy joven. Y en segundo lugar, Estados Unidos está muy lejos y es inmensamente grande. ¿Como vas a poder encontrarlo?" ("Look, daughter, you are not going to go alone to look for Juan. In the first place, you are very young. And secondly, the United States is far away and is immensely big. How will you be able to find him?")

"Bueno no sé exactamente," she replied. ("Well, I don't know exactly.")

Maria was then around forty-five or fifty years old. She and her husband had traveled all over the United States and Canada, whenever he was able to take a vacation, as he had a good job as general manager of the General Popo factory, a big manufacturer of car and truck tires. His name was Carlos Holman.

Carlos and Maria asked Lupe, "¿qué papeles vas a presentar en el Consulado Americano?" ("What papers are you going to present to the American Consulate?")

Lupe said, "Tengo esta carta de mi hermana." ("I have this letter from my sister.") She showed them the letter that her sister Teresa had sent years earlier. They then told her, "Regreseta a La Piedad por tu certificado de nacimiento y cualquier otra documentación legal que puedas encontrar." ("Go back to La Piedad for your birth certificate and any other legal documentation you can find.")

46

They also asked if Lupe planned on going alone to find Juan and were pleased to know that she could arrange to have some help from her older sister. "Pero," ¿qué pasa con la frontera? Si por alguna razón te rechazan, entonces estás sola." ("But," they added, "what about the border? If they turn you back for some reason, then you are all alone.")

"Bueno, no había pensado en eso, tengo fe en Dios y creo que todo saldrá bien, no tengo otra opción." ("Well, I hadn't thought about that. I have faith in God, and I believe that everything will turn out well. I do not have any other option.")

Trina and Lupe returned to La Piedad to collect birth certificates and anything else that might help them. By this time, Trina wanted to join in this journey to the United States. Once again, they arrived at the home of Maria and Carlos. The next morning, Carlos took them in his newly purchased car. He had acquired it from a television performer of Los Polivoces, a famous two-person comedy team whose show, *El Show de Los Polivoces*, was extremely popular throughout Mexico at that time. He took Lupe and Trina to get Mexican passports, and on the following day, he took them to the American Embassy at five o'clock in the morning.

They were standing on the Calle Progresso (Street of Progress) sidewalk, waiting to enter the graceless, fortress-like embassy building as the sun arose. A hundred people or more were already lined up ahead of them. The applicants were allowed to enter in groups of twenty-five people at a time. Trina and Lupe were the only ones given permits to enter the United States in their group of twenty-five. Their permits meant that they could enter or leave the United States at any time. In a journey with so many struggles, this

47

encounter with officialdom was easier than they dreamed possible.

They returned to La Piedad with their permits in hand, intent on going to the United States. A letter from Juan was waiting for them. He had sent eighty dollars, roughly equal to a year's salary in Mexico at that time. To Lupe, these dollars felt like they had come from heaven. Lacking a telephone, she replied to Juan via telegram, letting him know that she had received the money. The telegram became more expensive with each additional letter or word, so she was as succinct as possible: They had arranged for passports and wondered if he wanted them to go to where he was.

Juan was in Lodi, California, an agriculturally based city of about twenty-eight thousand people about forty miles south of the state's capital, Sacramento. He was living in a labor camp there and earning money *trabajando en la pisca de uvas* (vineyard worker).

Juan responded quickly with a plan: Lupe and Trina would fly to Tijuana, the border city just below San Diego. A cousin would meet them. Trina would then return to La Piedad, and the cousin would deliver Lupe to Lodi, a five-hundred-mile drive.

Lupe was thrilled to be headed to the United States, and especially to the state of California, the home of the Kennedys (she thought they lived there; she thought all famous people lived in Hollywood), Elvis Presley, and many other great stars whom she saw years before in Rosario's backyard screenings. She wondered if Elvis might live near Lodi.

Despite the joyous butterflies in her stomach, Lupe worried about leaving her young kids behind. But she knew it was in the family's best interest: Juan could never return to the Ranch in Mexico. She and her husband had to prepare and save money so that their children could also be brought to the US for their own safety and security. It's not what she wanted; ideally, she would still be at the Ranch with Rosario, Juan, and the kids. However, this was how life dealt her cards, and she accepted it. She felt she was making the right decisions for her family at that moment in time.

Lupe had heard many fabulous stories about the United States, its many opportunities, and the successes achieved by immigrants who had already gone there, including her older sister, Teresa, as well as her husband and children in the city of Salinas, located on Highway 101, also known as El Camino Real (The Real Way).

Lupe dreamed of what she and Juan could accomplish together in the United States. Her hopes expanded, along with her emotions and dreams. In September 1970, a strange car arrived, and Lupe and Trina kissed and hugged the kids goodbye. The kids watched their mom and grandmother get in the car and drive away. The children were left behind with Raquel. In their minds, they could not understand why Mom and Grandma were going far away to join Dad, whom they hadn't seen in what seemed to be years. They were confused, and their youthful minds wondered if their mother would ever come back again. Did this mean they would not see their mom in years, too?

The two women rendezvoused with the cousin. He took Lupe to Lodi, riding there on roadways of astounding size. She saw manicured lawns, stucco homes, white picket

49

fences, and beautifully lit tall buildings unlike anything she had encountered in Michoacán. In the time it took to reach Lodi, Lupe saw more luxury cars and trucks than she had seen before in her whole life.

They arrived late on a Saturday. Lupe was exceedingly happy to be reunited with her long-lost husband. She expected to be outraged with him, but on seeing him, her heart moved away from its feelings of abandonment, and instead, she felt so relieved to be at his side once again. That had been her goal, to find the father of her children. She felt that God had heard her prayers, that He wanted them to find each other after more than six months were lost in searching, hoping, and wondering. It had seemed an eternity.

On Sunday, Lupe went into Lodi to buy clothes rugged enough for fieldwork. Juan had explained to her the type of job they would have and made her realize that however prominent they may have been in Mexico, running their own business or occupying any place of importance whatsoever was not possible now. First, there was the language barrier. While working long and hard hours, as many as their strength allowed, they also had to acquire a difficult new language. Secondly, Juan had only a little bit of US professional work experience, and Lupe lacked it entirely. They had to grab the bottom rung of the ladder and hold on as if their lives depended on their determined grip. Lupe was okay with their current situation and felt at ease next to Juan, who was strong and confident.

On Monday, Lupe began working alongside her husband, gathering her first daily portion of California's enormous annual grape harvest. She rose before the sun was up and dragged herself over the still-damp dirt in the vineyard,

50

moving efficiently from vine to vine, stretching into the canopies of grape leaves and vines to gather the bunches.

They were heavy, especially when her arms were fully extended away from her torso. Meanwhile, tiny flies were abundant in their leaves. Competing with the human intruders for the rich sugars inside each grape, they swarmed straight into her face.

Lupe learned to maneuver quickly in each section of the rows where she worked, cutting the bunches in a patterned movement that went upward, to the side, and then down. She filled numerous boxes, working while crouching and moving her body in unaccustomed ways.

Her first day was epically tiring, but she was so happy to be with Juan. Everything felt so right, and the money they were paid felt awfully good.

Lupe arrived in California with many illusions and an unshakable desire to work as hard as she could and earn as much money as possible. Thrilled that her family would one day be together in California and working for citizenship, she decided that "Trabajando duro aquí significa ganar buen dinero, y con dinero no se sufre." ("Hard work here means earning good money, and with money you do not suffer.")

This thought soothed her heart from the pain of being away from her children, her parents, and her homeland. She held tight to it because her children, parents, sisters —in one simple word, her family—always came into her mind and her heart.

The first checks Juan and Lupe earned were sent to their children so that they could eat well and feel happy. Their children had been scared. Life had given them and their parents a firm shaking. Because of what the family went through and all the events that followed the death of their patriarch, the kids never had a real childhood while they were in Mexico. Alberto and Chayo, were two little adult men who, at their youthful age, had gone out and found work to earn money to buy food for their younger siblings. Because their family did not have a cent, they worked instead of playing like the other children their age.

In Mexican culture, the interconnectedness of one's family is honored and sustained at a devotional level, seldom seen in the USA. Lupe believed in her heart that one day she would bring her children to this new country, where marvelous things might happen in their lives.

8. Migrant Status

Grape-picking season gradually waned. By mid-September, Lodi's annual festival to celebrate the completion of harvest was underway. While others celebrated, Juan and Lupe moved on to picking walnuts and other nearby crops.

Walnuts are harvested with a big machine that shakes the trees. All the nuts in their shells fell to the ground while Juan and Lupe walked behind the machines and picked them up.

Olive season came along next, followed by oranges, lemons, and peaches.

Oranges, lemons, and peaches are heavy and dirty work, and they are painful too. The oranges come in different varieties, like many other fruits. The Sotos pick this fruit throughout the year, whose regular picking time comes perfectly between the apple and cherry seasons. The heavy, dusty oranges are picked with scissors. Lupe and Annabel have scars along the side of their calves to show the damage the sharp scissors can do. The oranges are collected on a heavy cloth sack cinched across their back. The fruit is dumped into a wooden bin and later delivered to the packing house in a diesel truck. The lemon branches had thorns that left scratches everywhere on Lupe's and Juan's bodies. They had to wear a special heavy sleeve on their arms, but it did not guarantee protection. As Lupe and Juan pushed their way into the trees looking for the fruit, they suffered pokes and pricks from the thorny branches. They did not feel the pain at the moment, only when they got back to their camps and showered. At night, they found themselves rubbing alcohol on their accumulated scratches.

After a while, they got more skilled at maneuvering around the tree in a way that would minimize the pricking and scratching.

The beautiful and sweet peaches that needed harvesting were no less difficult to pick. They look pretty on the trees, but to get them from the tree to the box was intimidating. The peach fuzz proved to be a dangerously itchy kind of skin torture, combined with the hot 100-degree temperature, making these a nightmare. No type of clothing can protect a field worker from it. The farm labor contractor told Juan and Lupe not to scratch the first itch—otherwise, they would itch and scratch all day long. But they really could not avoid the itch. At the end of a peach picking day, their bodies were dirty, sticky from the peach juice, and red from peach fuzz irritation. Bathing in rubbing alcohol at the end of the day made peach harvest a serious way of earning a buck. It also made Juan long for the drinkable kind of alcohol, another itch that proved difficult to conquer.

The migrant trail began when the California harvests were finished, Lupe and Juan ventured into the Pacific Northwest. Cherry trees were waiting there. First, they picked the Chelan variety, followed soon by Bing, and then Rainier and Sweetheart. Cherry picking filled their time and their pockets until early fall, when the apples of Oregon, Washington, and Idaho were hanging heavy on branches.

Though fate had dictated that a golden boy from Michoacán must now be a migrant field hand, Juan was not meek. He was unafraid of anything or anybody. However, he

54

held his anger inside all through the workday. Then, when evening came, he could assuage it with alcohol.

Juan wanted to be respected by the landowners and labor contractors, so he didn't drink until after work. Then, he would finish a bottle of wine over supper, sleep a few hours, and report to work before sunrise again. He had not undertaken treatment for his alcoholism, and he never would.

Lupe and Juan lived for a time in Gridley with Juan's uncle, who was a farm labor contractor and made very good money—enough for a big house, fancy cars, jewelry, and other material things. Juan thought that perhaps agriculture was a good business to be in. He was making steady money, and within a few months, he and Lupe sent Trina enough money to buy the family a little house in La Piedad.

Juan wanted to return to Mexico between harvest seasons, seeing their children for half of a year, profitably working the harvest in between. But Lupe knew that being away from her children that much would be emotionally untenable for her and that any return to Michoacán would expose her husband and family to great risk.

Lupe insisted on staying in the US, harvesting fruits and vegetables from daybreak until the gray of the evening, through spring and summer and fall, and then finding other work in between. For example, there were olive and citrus fruit picking and processing jobs in California's Central Valley. Those jobs could run all the way into winter. By staying stateside longer, she and Juan could more quickly save up the funds they needed to make the USA their young family's new home.

But for all its milk and honey, the USA was a land with contradictions. Lupe and Juan had already experienced its confusing mixture of tremendously welcome opportunities, along with no small number of cold-hearted people whose narrowed eyes signaled a deep contempt for brown-skinned immigrants.

SOTO FAMILY

Migrant Trail

Date	Location	Activity	Notes
May	Lodi and Stockton in California	Picking Cherries	Picking a variety of cherries.
June - July	Idaho, Oregon and Washington	Picking Cherries	Picking a variety of cherries.
July - August	Idaho	Onion and Corn Fields	Harvesting onion seeds and corn tassel pulling.
August - September - October	Idaho	Corn Cannery	The kids began working at the American Fine Foods in Oregon as early as age 14, legally.
October - November	Idaho, Oregon	Apple Picking	Picking a variety of apples.
November	California	School	The kids went back to school.
November	California	Picking Olives	Picking Olives during the weekends.
December - May	California	Picking Citrus	Oranges, lemons, mandarines, grapefruits
December - May	California	Packing Houses/Sheds	As the kids grew older, they took jobs in local fruit and vegetable packing houses.

9. American-Born Brothers

Lupita and Juanito, the youngest children living in La Piedad, called their grandmother Mama Trina, believing she was their real mother.

Trina and Raquel cared for the six siblings. Trina was very modern in her thinking and loved being thoroughly involved in their lives. She often drew them into "committee meetings" in which they made group decisions.

Along with some helpful relatives, Trina prepared Jell-O and homemade donuts for the kids to sell around their neighborhood. She kept the money in a cigar box that she stashed in an armoire in the living room in a lockable compartment. However, down the street, a boy with the nickname El Viejito (the little old man) was given to him because of a disease that caused him to really look like a little old man.

El Viejito's family had a similar piece of furniture, and one day, Anabel and Primo learned that its key could open the armoire used to secure savings. Once in a while, Anabel would use that rogue key to liberate a few pesos, though hopefully never enough to draw suspicion. A small neighborhood grocery store sold Pan Bimbo (the local equivalent to Wonder Bread) by the slice. The kids ran across an empty, dirt-filled soccer field, leaving a grubby cloud behind to get to the smallest shack, resembling a tiny grocery store around the corner. It was one of the luxuries Anabel bought to treat her sister and brothers. Eaten plain, the bread was a piece of heaven.

Trina also bought the family Pan Bimbo slice by slice. It cost more that way in the long run but kept more pesos in the home in the short term. As many poor people have learned through the ages, poverty costs a great deal.

In La Piedad, there was so much poverty and a scant chance of ever getting above it. People seemed always to be talking about their dreams of crossing the US border and finding opportunity. The family's neighbors and relatives often spoke of the coyotes; the people found up near the borderline who specialized in sneaking Mexicans into the USA. Some of those stories were cautionary, telling of people who paid money to coyotes only to find themselves caught by the well-armed Border Patrol agents and sent back home. Or, worse, being abandoned by their coyote, who had panicked and left them locked in the back of a two-ton truck to die of dehydration. Another story told to the children said that a young man who crossed the border on foot over the desert managed to reach the USA, but the ordeal made him deathly sick, so he died alone in the promised land.

The children began to wonder if maybe moving to the US was not so grand after all.

It then cost about $500 for a person to get smuggled through the border or led on foot in the dark of night from the Tijuana desert to the San Ysidro, California, point of entry. The sons and daughters of Lupe and Juan Soto had become used to the poverty that cruelly engulfed them and wondered why the grownups around them kept talking about their hopes of entering the United States.

Meanwhile, in the States, Juan and Lupe had created two new little brothers. George was born in Stockton, and Manuel, nicknamed Meño in Oroville, a foothills town lying between Chico and Yuba City.

Lupe decided to visit her children in Mexico and introduce them to their new little brothers. Unfortunately, their stay was so short that the younger kids—Juanito, Lupita, and Prieto—didn't form lasting memories of the event.

First, George developed a fever accompanied by dysentery. Then Manuel, less than a year old, was stricken with the same illness. When he became lethargic, they rushed him to the hospital, but during the car ride, he stopped breathing. Trina took him in her arms and performed CPR.

At the hospital, the doctor told Lupe and Juan that they must get back home to California. There was no cure for them in Mexico. If they didn't go back, the infant boys would die.

As soon as they crossed the border, Manuel ceased vomiting. A US doctor prescribed medicine for the boys, and they bounced back to normal immediately.

Manuel and George grew up in Gridley. They were in daycare while Lupe and Juan worked, and sometimes a neighbor babysat for them. The babysitter saw how hard Lupe worked, and so she took very good care of the kids. When Lupe picked them up after a long day of work, both kids would be freshly showered, and their clothes cleaned and ironed.

Lupe and Juan soon moved to Lindsay, where they took a small apartment on Sweetbriar Avenue. By the time George and Manuel were around three and four years old, Chayo and Alberto arrived in the US. The apartment was too small for their family, so Lupe and Juan decided to rent a home on nearby Blue Gum Street.

Soon, Alberto and Chayo have grown up enough to join their parents on the migrant trail. Within two more years, the remaining children—Anabel, Primo, Lupita, and

Juanito—were brought to rejoin their parents and got to know their two new little brothers.

George and Manuel were five and six when they met their four older siblings again. The middle four children and the two younger brothers looked at each other like strange kids they'd never seen before. They had to learn to share the woman they all called mother. At first, it felt strange, but very soon, it felt good. Now, they all had more kids to play with on the playground and ride bikes with. Manuel was a cute little baby who got into everything, a complete handful. Lupe kept baby pictures of him all over the walls—a luxury she didn't get to enjoy when his older brothers and sisters were kids.

At last, they were together again, all under the same roof and a family of ten by this time. Eleven, actually, because Grandmother Trina was often part of the group, even during harvest seasons.

10. Blue Gum Avenue

When Lupita arrived in California, it felt to her as though she was meeting her parents for the first time, not to mention her new little brothers. Lupe looked so young and beautiful to Lupita. Her mother's skin was soft and supple, with a hint of gold. Her long, luscious, silky black hair was as thick as yarn, and her big brown eyes with long lashes accented Lupe's two dramatically prominent cheekbones and her slender nose.

To Lupita, her new California home on Blue Gum Avenue was a magical place surrounded by lush grass, radiant flowers, and beautiful trees, with the sun sweetly peeking through the swaying branches. All the colors were rich and flavorful. Everything seemed different to her young youthful eyes in a marvelous way. Pan Bimbo was now labeled Wonder Bread, and it came into their home in full-sized loaves, bought from a grocery store bigger than she'd ever imagined could exist. Mom toasted and buttered slices of it, sprinkling them lightly with sugar, and the flashbacks the newly arrived Soto kids had to the danger and poverty surrounding them in Mexico instantly evaporated. Buttered toast was a heaven-sent sign that life was now wonderfully different. How could it get any better?

With the addition of a new food called peanut butter, as it turned out. It went great with bread, toasted or plain, and also filled the miniature culverts of celery stalks. Many other superb, tempting new things awaited in their mother's nearby kitchen. The youngsters sat on the steps of the back porch, admiring a prospering flower and vegetable garden.

A yellow bicycle leaned against the fence. Alberto and Chayo had outgrown it, so the yellow bike was now eagerly ridden by Anabel and Primo, as well as Juanito—who decided to Americanize his name to Johnny. All three quickly mastered the two-wheeler. In time, Lupita found the courage to pedal it inside the fence's boundaries, coached by her trusted siblings. Older sister Anabel was adventurous, riding the bike beyond the compound of the fence just as the boys did. She pedaled all around the quiet neighborhood on the paved roads, which made the tires whistle as they rolled at speed.

The old bike's frame finally gave way to stress cracks that appeared where its steel tubes were welded together at the factory. They got rewelded, and the much-loved bike kept serving its newest masters. Then, one day, Johnny crashed it against the fence, and the bike broke in half. The kids watched sadly as their yellow bike was placed in the trash can. But it was soon replaced with a fancy ten-speed.

This new bike was so big and fancy that only the older boys felt brave enough to ride it. Lupita and Anabel had to find another way to entertain themselves. Their mom bought them lots of American-style toys, including Barbie dolls and roller skates. Lupita found a Native American doll very interesting and different, and she took it to school for Show and Tell, even though Lupe tried to influence her to display one of the blonde Barbies.

Lindsay was a friendly city. Lupe and Juan left the car unlocked, both day and night. On hot summer nights, the family slept with the doors to the house open and only the screen door closed. This way, the house would be cooler in the morning, and it would take longer for the summer heat—

temperatures above one hundred degrees were not unusual—
to become stifling inside.

The house on Blue Gum also felt a little more magical
when open doors and windows allowed the wind to blow the
gauzy curtains softly in the evening air. Lupe and Juan rented
this house for a couple of years, paying rent over the summer
months even though they were away, working the harvests,
because they wanted the treasured house available upon their
return from the Northwest.

Lupe deemed it important that her kids blend into
American culture. She exposed them to hot dogs and
hamburgers. She encouraged them to watch *The Brady
Bunch*, an American TV show of a large, blended family that
aired in the 1970s, and *Happy Days,* an American television
show displaying American teenagers and their high school
friends. She introduced her children to the fabled Kennedys,
as well as Elvis Presley, Barbara Streisand, Jane Fonda, and
John Wayne. They were sent to school with stamped-tin lunch
boxes painted colorfully with Wonder Woman, Superman,
and other American heroes. They soon had a plethora of
crayons, coloring books, and new clothes, so they would be
dressed sharply like the *Brady Bunch* kids. Lupe hoped they
would assimilate quickly and be spared the sidelong "stink
eye" looks she had experienced as an outsider. She also
instructed firmly against drugs, alcohol, and cigarettes. They
would undo all the hard work and striving that underlied the
family's escape from unpredictable enemies who threatened
their lives back in Michoacán.

"Ser un pilar para la sociedad," Lupe said to her
offspring. ("Be a pillar for society.") "Ten compasión y
respeto para toda la humanidad, independientemente de cómo

te traten y te miren algunas personas. Este es un nuevo comienzo en un gran país. Da más de lo que recibes. Hay que ser agradecidos." ("Have compassion and respect for all humanity, regardless of how some people treat you and look at you. This is a new beginning in a great country. Give more than what you receive. Be grateful.")

Lupita was excited to meet her father for the first time again. She longed for a father figure, as her mother insisted, although she did not really understand the emotions she was feeling at the time. She wanted him to be like the father she once saw in Mexico when she was playing there with one of her girlfriends. The girl wore the prettiest pink dress, lined with soft ruffles. Her hair was in tight curls, just like Shirley Temple's in the movies. As her father approached, the little girl immediately stopped playing. She got up and ran in his direction with her arms lifted into the air. His big daddy hands caught her tiny arms, and up into the air, she went, again and again, her curls bouncing sweetly every time. She giggled and laughed the entire time. Then she ran around him and crawled through his legs. Her father grabbed her and tossed her into the air above his head. Her ringlets bounced up and down in time with her happy giggles.

Lupita wished for a daddy who could do that acrobatic play with her. Where was this person, this father figure, to swing her up and down while they both laughed and were so happy?

Her reunion with Juan was truly a source of joy. He could do all the magical daddy things she could ever want. But at that young age, she didn't understand that her father was in some respects a struggling man, still haunted by how suddenly his fate had changed a few short years before and

65

how he wished he was again the golden child of his father and mother.

11. But I Love School

Because they were a strong team, from the parents to the children, from the oldest to the youngest, the family was able to save as much as $50,000 per migrant season. Fifty thousand dollars in 1977 is equivalent to $250,000 today. That works out to somewhere around forty dollars a day per person, which doesn't seem like much until you consider that each person was working as a member of a devoted family team, and so their strength and their income was a team effort, with every single team member giving their all.

For the kids, though, this came at the cost of missing almost a quarter of their school year. Their loss of classroom time was doubly expensive. They had a lot of catching up to do to learn the English skills that would be key to other academic advancements.

Before their Grandfather Rosario's tragic and violent death, Alberto had been ready for Educacion Media Superior (equivalent to tenth through twelfth grades in high school) grade at a private military school and was destined to be educated to become a medical doctor. He was the family's firstborn male, and so he was expected to grow into a leadership role in the family. His projected tuition had already been paid in full by his grandfather. Two of his cousins, whose families remained in Mexico, eventually entered the medical school that was prepaid by Rosario. One that they knew of became a dentist. But Alberto and the next-oldest brother, Chayo, instead became the first of Juan and Lupe's kids to move to the US.

Upon his arrival, Alberto was assigned by school authorities to be in ninth grade. His English skills were not yet well polished, and bilingual instruction was not yet offered in California schools. So, Alberto was advanced enough for the senior class but was required to enter as a freshman.

Chayo, Rosario's namesake, started his California schooling in the eighth grade. Both he and Alberto had been hard workers and important contributors to the family's finances, but Alberto found it more difficult to sync up with the norms and customs of his new surroundings and the English tongue. Chayo was a very social person, very likable and trusting, and he embraced the new culture around him with enthusiasm. He immediately fell in love with America and everything it had to offer. It had freedom, safety, and security, which were very important to Chayo. Those aspects were important to the entire family, but Chayo really held onto those pieces. All his classes were in English, and nothing made sense to him until he joined high school because by that time, he was more exposed to the language. Alberto and Chayo realized in high school that they had already learned the material back in Mexico, but the lack of English language was holding them back. Chayo's grades were poor at best, and it did not help that he and Alberto worked all the time and had to forgo learning in the classroom. In addition to working the cherry and apple harvest up north, they picked the local olives, oranges, lemons, and grapes throughout the school year. Both missed classes all the way up to December, increasing their difficulties in keeping up at school.

In March and all the way until the family headed to the cherries in early May, Chayo and Alberto were out in the fields at 5:00 a.m. picking oranges in the dark using the truck lights for luminosity. They headed home with just enough time to shower and go directly to class. After school they both scurried to the field until midnight picking oranges to the lights of the trucks helping Juan and Lupe bring money into the household.

Anabel started school in the fifth grade. She did not understand a word of what the other kids were saying in the schoolyard that first morning. When she walked into her assigned classroom, she was met by a tall, blonde, thin lady with big, beautiful blue eyes. Her teacher wanted Anabel to write something down. She looked directly into the new girl's brown eyes and asked, "Where is your pencil?"

Realizing that Anabel needed translation, the teacher enlisted help from a boy who spoke Spanish. And so, the first thing Anabel learned was that *lapiz* meant "pencil," and vice versa. As the day went on, and as the weeks and months went by, Anabel learned a huge new supply of words. She discovered that she loved this new school and was excited to be learning the English language. It would take her two years to get comfortable with English and its many twists, turns, and numerous exceptions to rules. Why did *save* rhyme with *grave*, but not with *have*? Why did *have* sound just the same as *halve*, yet it meant something entirely different? And then why didn't *salve* sound like *save*? English was so puzzling that many native-born speakers struggled to absorb its contradictions.

Juanito started first grade in the same school as Lupita. Juanito was quiet and very observant. Lupita and Juanito waited patiently in the office while Lupe registered the kids. Juanito was quite calm about the whole thing and said he would pick up the English language quickly (and he really did). Once the adults were finished with the paperwork, Lupita and Juanito got escorted to their classrooms. They walked down the open corridor and were separated in different directions. Lupita joined him at recess, where they had the pleasure of getting introduced to the very popular merry-go-round. They waited patiently for two open spaces on the wheel. They rode for the very first time in their lives— what a joy. They spent all of their first school recess watching the sky spin.

Lupita met her first teacher. Mrs. Cooper was an older American lady who was thin and well-groomed and taught second grade.

Lupita watched Mrs. Cooper hold a deeply serious-seeming conversation with a Mexican-American woman who served as an assistant teacher. Later, the Mexican-American woman explained: "Mrs. Cooper is glad to see you and is grateful that you are neat and clean, even if you don't speak English."

At home that evening, Anabel and Prieto shared all the brand-new English words they'd learned in one day: "One, two, three, four, five. Yellow, green, red, black, and white."

Blue was Lupita's first English word.

Mrs. Cooper's classroom had a tall wooden object with a mahogany front and sides, which contrasted with a wide swath of little black-and-white blocks across the width of its front. Lupita had never seen such an object but was told that its name was *piano*. Mrs. Cooper asked her if she'd care to stay in the classroom during recess so she might learn to play the piano. Following Mrs. Cooper's instructions, Lupita touched some of the piano's keys with her little fingers. It made the most beautiful sound she had ever heard. When Christmas arrived a few weeks later, she was able to play a song called "Jingle Bells" in front of all her American classmates.

Most of their Anglo classmates didn't understand why the Soto boys and girls were absent at the start of the school year *and* at the end. The siblings also found it embarrassing to admit that they had been out of class because they'd been trekking to orchards and vineyards all around California and beyond, working as a family in orchards and fields for the sake of mutual survival. Their loss of classroom time was doubly expensive. However, this way of earning a living comes at a cost for the kids. While harvesting, they miss almost a quarter of their school year. The loss of the classroom is a sword with two sharp edges. They have so much catching up to do, particularly in learning English skills, and they need those skills in order to stoke their academic advancement. They simply have to struggle to keep up, a process that will be more demanding every year. Catching up requires all the Soto kids to work harder than everyone else. The older boys' GPAs suffer proportionately, but so do the GPAs of the younger siblings. The Soto kids are handicapped by having fewer weeks of school time, just as any children would be, native-born or immigrant.

By the time some of the kids reach high school, special programs have been made available to make education easier for immigrant children. For example, they can do their schoolwork in Spanish, aided by Spanish-speaking tutors. But by this time, the kid's English proficiency is too high for eligibility to those helpful programs. Other Mexican

American kids end up with better GPAs and even graduate with honors without attaining their level of English fluency.

In spite of it all, Lupita loved school for its opportunities to learn and to connect with friends, just like Anabel.

12. Home Sweet Home

The children came to America at the start of the cherry season in California. Spring was well on its way to becoming summer, so the orchards in Idaho, Oregon and Washington would bloom next, right after the California crop. When they did, the team known as Juan and Lupe Soto would be there with their family crew, ready to pick their share of the annual hundreds of tons of sweet cherries.

Other kids would remain in their classes for a few more weeks, but this was when Juan and Lupe would pick the Soto kids up from school and hit the road. They left their school and the town of Lindsay in a family vehicle that their kids decided to call El Tabique. That means "the brick." It was a stodgy old Dodge pickup, dating from just after World War Two. The factory-applied red paint, some three decades old, had become seriously sunbaked. That gave the truck—which would become the whole family's main dwelling place for the next six months—the variegated red-brown-pink hues of ancient terracotta.

As soon as the family hit 99, the 425-mile highway that ran the full length of the San Joaquin Valley, the old Dodge thumped and bumped until Juan steered it to the side of the road. A tire had gone flat. Juan had packed a toolbox in case the truck developed any mechanical issues, but for some reason, he neglected to bring along a jack in case of a flat tire.

The kids and grown-ups searched the highway side and found discarded bricks to stack between the ground and the truck's frame. Then they took turns digging underneath the flat tire until they'd excavated a big hole. The bad tire came off, a good one went on in its place, and the Sotos were on their way again.

Mechanical problems cropped up at various times along the highways. The six-cylinder engine would sometimes run so hot that they had to let El Tabique sit by the side of the road, steaming, until they could safely slake the radiator's thirst with the extra water they carried in plastic one-gallon milk jugs. Its sticky transmission linkage sometimes needed a whack with a wrench before it decided to go into second gear. Juan attended to the mechanical needs of El Tabique's primitive flathead six-cylinder engine and balky stick-shift transmission over that span of time in the cheapest and most expeditious way possible. Before any clothes or other necessary things, his toolbox was the first item to be packed. A master mechanic, a *maestro mecanico*, was a highly esteemed person in Mexican culture. They kept cars, trucks, and other old machinery able to do their vital jobs a little longer. Those skills could save lives and money, too.

The Soto family and all the belongings they would need for the next six months were already packed into El Tabique by the end of the day's classes, so the entourage headed straight from school to Lodi, the first stop in their pilgrimage. The older brothers teased their young siblings, claiming the family would move to Idaho after the cherries were all picked in Lodi and Stockton. Lupita couldn't understand why they would ever leave their magical house on Blue Gum Street, but at the same time, she was happy to be bouncing down Highway 99 toward an all-family adventure.

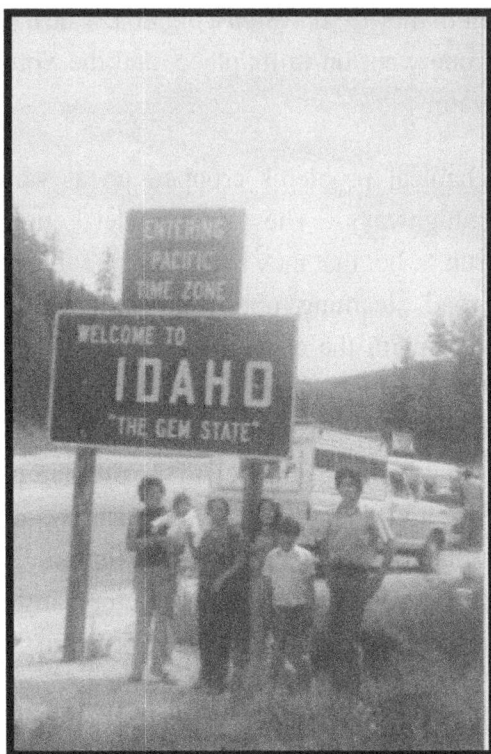

But in fact, Idaho really was slated to be their home during the winter of 1977–78. The kids were enrolled in the local Caldwell schools rather than returning to Lindsay. Their classmates were nearly all Caucasian. Lupita was the only Latina in her class, and alongside her Anglo classmates, she came off as vibrant and outspoken. In November, the Soto kids had their first snow experience. They took joy in spontaneous snowball fights. They giddily caught falling snowflakes on their tongues, and then collected a dishful apiece, on which they poured sweet syrup to make a *raspado,* a treat they'd enjoyed in Mexico. (To their new Idaho schoolmates and friends, this inexpensive delight was known as a sno-cone.)

The family spent the New Year of 1977 in Caldwell. Alberto and Chayo were grown up, further along than the other kids in becoming Americanized. Their pants had flapping, bell-bottomed legs, and their polyester shirts shone just like the ones John Travolta wore in the hit disco-themed movie *Saturday Night Fever*, dancing to "Stayin' Alive" by the Bee Gees.

The family owned a big record player on a stand. It played disco hits almost daily. Chayo and Alberto sang to *Don't Stop Believing* by Journey and danced Travolta-style to Bee Gees hits to get ready for a night out. The disco in Caldwell was really popular, flashing its bright, colorful lights by night, though empty and lonely during the day. It sat across the street from the laundromat the family went to every weekend to keep their clothes clean.

After the cherry season, cannery and apple harvest wound down in the winter, work in Idaho proved scarce. One day, Juan took Chayo on a business trip to Yuma, Arizona. A gringo, Jim Pelican who admired Juan's skill at handling work crews contacted him to offer a field supervisor position. But first he had to show that he could put together a work crew of thirty people to fill the lemon-picking jobs.

Juan and Chayo scoured local grocery stores, laundromats, and other local businesses looking for job candidates. They had no experience with the Arizona job market and zero connections and networks. They turned up none and decided to return to Idaho. Juan decided to make his way back up to Idaho through the little town of Lindsay. Juan and Chayo spent a couple of days visiting relatives and learning about the small friendly city. When they arrived back in Idaho, he presented the idea to leave the cold snow in

76

Idaho. It had become clear that California's great winter weather ensured year-round work possibilities, so the family decided they must return.

Juan and Lupe decided to take little Meño with them to Lindsay in search of a house. They toured various homes in Lindsay and considered buying in Stockton and Salinas, where Lupe's sister Teresa owned several Mexican grocery stores named El Charito Market. Juan dreamed of one day buying a grocery store like the ones Teresa and her husband owned. During a neighbor's visit, a friend told Juan he was considering selling his home as he had his eyes fixated on another property.

Juan and Lupe toured the neighbor's Fresno Street home. It was older and somewhat small but well-maintained. A couple of rooms in the back might be good for the older boys. (And eventually, Alberto would use them for band practice.) On the same lot sat another small house, a one-bedroom casita, which the owners rented out.

Juan thought the Fresno Street house was a good buy. Lupe wished for a bigger home, one that in effect could fit the entire family. Juan proposed that the boys sleep in the casita. Then, after the boys were grown, they could rent it out for extra income.

The owner planned to put the house on the market for $39,000. Thanks to their constant penny-pinching, Juan and Lupe actually had that amount in cash.

Lupe argued that buying for cash would save them many thousands of dollars in interest payments over the next twenty years while they paid off the mortgage. But Juan had bold plans in mind to start a trucking company with his sons, requiring them to hold on to some of the family's cash reserves.

Juan's logic prevailed, and they moved the family into their new Lindsay home on Fresno Street. They had to pay a monthly installment of $231.39 in order to stay there.

Lupita was still a little girl, oblivious to the plans Lupe and Juan had devised for getting ahead and the sacrifices they made. She simply went along as the family flowed from one scene to another, seemingly without notice. One day she would be in a magical, whimsical house on Blue Gum Avenue. The next day might find her in the middle of a wet, cold cherry orchard as the sun prepared to set. Yet, another day she would be in a classroom where all the other kids were Caucasian, just before she would be saying goodnight to her family as they all got ready to sleep beneath an army surplus tent in the foothills of the Sierra Nevada range. For the Soto family, life moved quickly from one scene to another—as it had done ever since the untimely death of their patriarch, Rosario Soto, years before.

When Lupita was in fourth grade in Idaho, she and four classmates were selected to write and perform a play about the Lewis and Clark Expedition of 1804–06. She was slated to play Sacajawea, the female Indian guide who was so vital to the expedition's success. They worked together on the script, made costumes, and created a life-sized two-dimensional replica of the expedition's canoe to use as a prop. The students practiced every chance they had, even during recess and lunch. Lupita was supercharged with excitement as the big day approached.

That day never came for her. Instead, on sudden notice, the family packed their belongings into El Tabique for another leg of the Soto Expedition. No advance notice, no time for goodbyes. Leaving friends behind, they set off for Lindsay to move into their newly purchased home.

The Soto expeditioners arrived in Lindsay in December 1978. Celebrating Christmas and a new home felt like enough gifts to keep the family going all year round. Juan and Lupe made it extra special that year by surprising the kids with a decorated tree and lots of presents under the tree on Christmas morning. Since that year, Christmases have remained big events at the Soto house on Fresno Street, beginning at Thanksgiving and going until New Year's Day.

Throughout the rest of the year, on their few free weekends, Lupe made sure the kids attended church on Sundays. Lindsay was a small town. Everybody knew everybody. It was safe and comfortable, a great place for bringing up a family. Kids played out in the street until dusk ended their games; parents left keys in the ignitions of their cars, with windows down and doors unlocked. Neighbors brought their leftovers to feed other neighbors. They did not complain if music was joyously loud at night, and inviting neighbors over for impromptu carne asada, which means grilled beef or BBQ, became a ritual for celebrating every one of life's little wins: a Little League championship, good grades, birthdays. A holiday, carne asada, they got company, carne asada. Random Saturdays and Sundays just because it was a nice day, carne asada. Everyone participated; the oldest kids fired up the grill, sometimes two grills. Lupe prepared the main dish, and the daughters-in-law brought side dishes and dessert. There was always lots of food and happiness in the Soto residence. No matter the occasion, the entire family showed up for these events.

Every Sunday, one family at a time, they show up at Lupe and Juan's home. The house filled up fast with grandkids running around in and out of the house, teenagers, sometimes still in their pajamas, sleepily trying to wake up on the couch. Grownups in the dining room set up table and, in the kitchen, cooking breakfast the most important meal of the day. Alberto and Lupe in the kitchen firing up the stove. The menu changed from menudo to carnitas, chorizo con huevos and handmade tortillas. Sometimes, the family had it all in one sitting. As the family grew, it was necessary to expand the menu. With grandchildren in the mix, Lupe catered to them with a special menu containing pancakes, waffles, omelets, burritos, and of course, handmade flour tortillas.

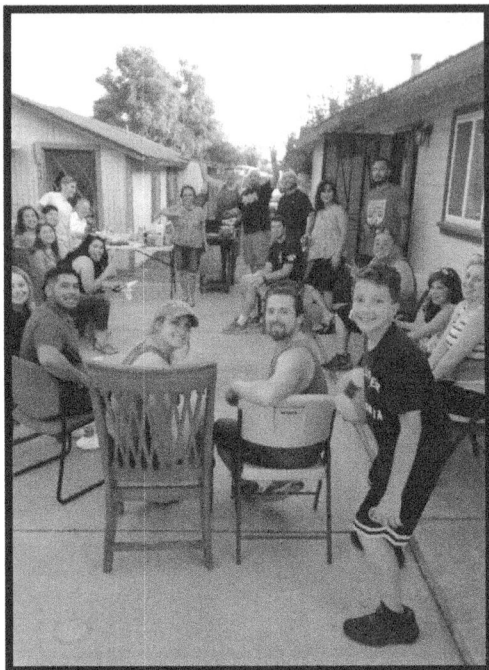

That same little house is now Lupe's, where her children and grandchildren can often be found gathered around her wooden table, being fed by the *abuelita* who, as a younger woman, fed her family and their coworkers on the migrant trail with burritos that were small miracles of flavor.

It's the place this tale began, the day a grown-up and married-with-children Lupita pays a visit and learns that her mother had begun writing down memories from her challenging life, in pencil, in modest notepads bought from a Lindsay drugstore.

13. It's All about the Journey

Every spring, year after year, Juan furnished the family's truck steel bed with boards and mattresses, then bolted its aluminum camper shell over the top before packing in all the clothes, cookware, and tools the traveling family would need for upcoming jobs. With extra care, he also loaded in an old portable black-and-white TV. This was for the fortunate nights when they shared the luxury of a single motel room, and electric power was waiting to make the old set come alive.

Juan drove the various highways they needed to travel to get them to the distant places where money grew on trees. Lupe sat next to him, most often with Mama Trina in the middle.

Anabel was wedged next to the door as the fourth occupant of a bench-style seat on which anything beyond two bodies was a crowd. Seven of the kids rode in the back of the truck, under the aluminum camper shell, which meant they were sharply cold in the winter and warm as a lidded cookpot in the summer. Every time they loaded back into it, they each took a particular territory. The older siblings always got the mattresses that lay on top of the boards. The boards themselves were lodged crosswise in the truck bed, creating a shelf, and those mattresses on top were definitely the best seats in the house, even without seat belts. The rest of them took up parcels of open space on the truck's bed. Lupita's back often hurt from slouching or lying on the unforgiving steel when she tried to nap.

Moving around in that tiny bit of rolling house was challenging, too, but it was the kind of pain and frustration the passengers could quickly forget because they had so much fun riding back there and being as noisy as they wanted to be.

Each journey began in Stockton and Lodi, where cherries waited to be picked. Once the family arrived at a work destination, they unloaded El Tabique. The old truck's contents were transferred into either a tent or, when one was available, a migrant camp shack. These shacks were often built from unpainted wooden planks that shrank with age and exposure, creating many passages for the night winds to come inside.

Labor camps in California have a history going back to the Dust Bowl and the Great Depression when a natural disaster drove untold numbers of Americans to work for their subsistence in California's agricultural lands. Labor camps—which were essentially newly built slums—were one answer to the housing crisis the migrant laborers faced. Eventually, a new group of impoverished laborers from Mexico and beyond "inherited" the labor camps.

For Juan and Lupe Soto and their children, staying at the labor camp meant living in a one-room shack with no inside walls, just the interior face of the outer wood-plank siding. Different spaces served as the kitchen, dining room, living room, and bedroom. But labor camp rent was very cheap. Sometimes, if the dirty and crammed units were owned by the rancher or the rancher's labor contractor, they may have been free of charge.

Restrooms and showers in these labor camps were communal spaces. After members of the family had showered, the 90- and 100-degree weather and the windborne dust of their surroundings soon had the Sotos gritting their teeth once again. There was no air conditioning, of course. But occasionally, the cabins had electricity, and Juan would plug in the small electric fan he'd packed in the truck.

Labor camps were mostly populated with married men, primarily from Mexico, though some others came to the migrant trail all the way from the Philippines. They worked the harvests from May to October and sent as much of their money home to their families as they could, honoring their obligations to the people they loved via long stretches of hard work at low pay. "Mucho trabajo, poco dinero" is how they ruefully described their shared situation.

There were many men who were alone, including married men whose families remained in Mexico or another country, and also lots of single men. Everyone called them *los solos* (the loners). Most of them would head back home to Mexico in the fall to live comfortably through the winter with their accrued earnings. Los solos were a happy bunch, often singing Mexican songs from Vicente Fernandez, Ramon Ayala, and romantic ballads from Luis Miguel, through the long hours of work, accentuating the verses every so often with a *grito,* the traditional Mexican addition of a spirited, high-pitched yelp. While the assembled workers were picking fruit all day, and in the moments between work and sleep at the labor camp, these sounds helped mark the passage of the day and signified the workers' determination to face tough conditions and carry on.

Sometimes, the family was blessed with a comfortable night's sleep in a shared motel room, like the Viking Motel on Cherokee Lane in Lodi. Twenty-three dollars bought a more comfortable night there. Sometimes, Juan and Lupe agreed that they could afford two rooms—one shared by the boys, the other just for the girls. For the Soto family's kids, an overnight stay in a motel was a sweet experience, the closest thing they would experience to the delights of a Disneyland trip.

By the late seventies and early eighties, the labor camps were outlawed. Conditions in the camps threatened workers' health, so, by extension, they jeopardized getting crops harvested.

In response to the absence of labor camp housing, motels aggressively raised their rates during harvest. A modest motel, one that might normally charge between $10 and $20 per night, might suddenly gouge the migrant laborers by charging as much as $200. In those same years, a Manhattan hotel suite would cost less per night than these drab motels in a small California town.

When rates were at their highest or when the motels were at maximum occupancy, Juan and Lupe rented the family a single room. The boys were sent to sleep in El Tabique while Mom, Dad, and Mama Trina shared their space with Anabel and Lupita. Sometimes, the boys stayed in the room, making their beds on the floor.

A motel stay meant little or no cooking and potentially the grand excitement of eating their evening meals at a fast-food restaurant. Not McDonald's or Burger king, but juicy, greasy, cheese hamburgers and fries from a nearby hamburger shack. The place served food that stained the paper bag within seconds. Some believed that it was the best hamburger joint in all of California. During the day, Lupe would bring a portable stove and a few pots and pans to the job site. She created a humble yet great workers' feast for her family. Every meal was carefully and thoughtfully planned. Some days, Juan bought a rotisserie chicken from a local deli, with a loaf of Wonder Bread to be used in place of tortillas and bottles of Coca-Cola to wash it down.

Back at the Viking Motel the next morning, an alarm would sound at 3:00 a.m. Lupe would jump up instantly and urge her sleepy family, "¡Ya es hora, levantensen!" (It's time, get up!).

If Juan got up right away, his kids did too. They knew from experience that they were at risk of an all-day tongue-lashing if they failed to respond. When Juan lay low, he was hung over from the alcohol he drank before bedtime. The kids took advantage, squeezing in a little more pillow time. Regardless of the situation, Lupe never gave up. The family heard her say, "El sol ya está bien salido y si no nos vamos nos perderemos toda la mañana." ("The sun is up, and if we don't get going, we will miss the entire morning.") Before long, they would comply. The frustration rang unmistakably in her voice.

While cooking breakfast, Lupe simultaneously packed their lunches with delicious *tacos de carne con chile y frijoles* (beef tacos with salsa and beans made with flour tortilla, which resembled miniature burritos that fit perfectly in the fist of your hand).

Soon, they were out in a cold, wet cherry orchard, standing groggily in line to be handed twelve- and sixteen-foot ladders and cinching buckets around their waists to catch the fruit as they picked. Trudging half-asleep through rows of trees at the crack of dawn, Lupita often wondered, "Why me?"

She wished she might return to a soft pillow, but Lupe pushed her crew on. The orchard was big, filled with lots of trees that lined up in rows as far as the eye could see. They walked down a path in the middle of the orchard, fully loaded with tools, reaching their first *seta* (set of trees). Little hands carried something: a ladder, food, water, a coffee thermos, or buckets.

Everyone wanted the best trees, and sometimes you would get lucky with good-yielding fruit trees, and other times you wouldn't. No one seemed to care if the trees were tall or short; all pickers were just after the fruit. Orchards varied in size, and the trees had similar characteristics. Some orchards had approximately 120 to 140 trees per acre; most orchards were ten to twenty acres. Younger trees yielded better quality fruit. Cherries needed five hundred hours of dormant cold weather to produce great crops; otherwise, it was a bad picking season. The younger the trees, the smaller their size.

The Soto team arrived at the picking site. The trees were hanging heavily with ripe fruit ready for the picking. Heavy branches yielded lots of fruit, which was telling them that it was going to be a good, profitable season. If the rain came in too soon, it could potentially ruin the quality of the fruit. The more fruit on the trees, the higher the opportunity for making more money. The field supervisor checked in on every family and gave them a card utilized to track the number of boxes collected for the day. Throughout the day, a truck drove down a tight dirt road between the trees, collecting the full boxes stacked neatly under the trees. Every full box was counted carefully, and the collection card was punched with a hole, indicating the number of boxes collected. Once they were counted, the cherry boxes were picked up and dumped in a big bin lined with plastic to take to wash in a shed in preparation for packing and selling to grocery stores and for juicing. Counting each box was key; it had to be precise and calibrated between the picker and the collector. Some people stood with a watchful eye over their boxes until the truck drove off. Some contractors liked to take fruit from fully filled boxes to top off other boxes, causing pickers to lose one to three boxes per day. You would see some bickering back and forth when greedy contractors were involved in the collection of boxes.

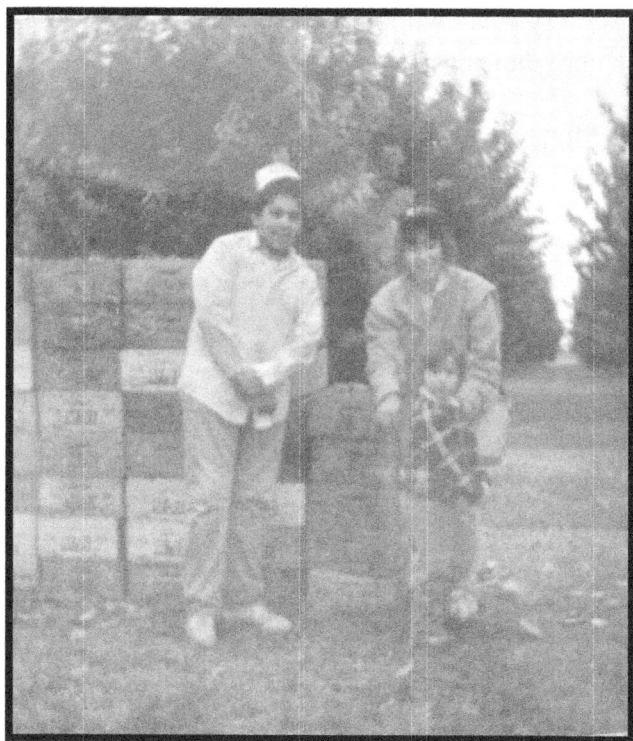

Picking was just plain tough on adults and kids alike. It required lifting and carrying a heavy twelve- to sixteen-foot wooden ladder or aluminum if you were lucky. The picker would place it in the tree, climb up, and pick the fruit until the bucket was full. You could only get off the ladder when the bucket was full to the rim, or the area of the tree had no more reachable fruit. While you were beyond the ladder's sixth step, your entire weight plus that of your bucket was pressed between your shin or hip and the ladder. You held on for all you were worth, hoping to the heavens that you didn't fall off. The buckets felt like lead weights when they were completely full. Your lower back and feet took a beating from all the climbing up and down. It was backbreaking work.

Every day's work was the prelude to the next and on and on until the crops were all in.

Money may grow on trees, but it does not collect itself.

Every filled box of cherries earned the Soto family close to three dollars. The first three or four boxes paid for the motel; the next few ensured everyone would eat. Beyond that lay an opportunity for carefully saved profit.

One day at the labor camp, Lupe allowed the youngest kids to sleep an extra hour under El Tabique's camper shell. They reported for work a little later in the morning, carrying water jugs, coffee, and the burritos that had been keeping warm on the car's dashboard. Suddenly, they saw many of the workers running away, with the men jumping off of tall ladders and running zig-zag past trees and fruit-filled boxes. They called out to the other workers, "La Migra! La Migra!"

The immigration authorities were conducting a raid. The Soto kids stopped dead in their tracks as workers ran around and past them. Some kids from the family groups got separated by the pursuing authorities, an event the kids would see frequently on the migrant trail. This made them grateful not to be subject to arrest, but they wished it was true for all their friends and coworkers.

Lupe was an excellent picker. So were the boys. Anabel kept up, too. Lupita tried her best, but in her young mind she drifted toward daydreams of a real vacation, like the kind that kids from her school would describe when she saw them again in October—maybe a plane flight to visit a grandma someplace far away, and afternoons spent swimming in a hotel's pool, or just a visit back home, wherever their family lived before coming to California. Instead, her summer was the same as the rest of her family, calling on their tired legs to take them up and down ladders, picking cherries, ending each day with sore muscles, dirty faces, and bruised shins. This was their pattern of life until the harvest seasons all ended. But, again, they were all together, sharing the good and the bad, and becoming very close as siblings.

Lupita and Juanito shared very similar dreams: go to college, get an office job with a big corporation, and make lots of money. Then, one day, they would buy Juan and Lupe a really nice house near a pretty beach.

Lupe was the one who would lead and push the family crew. She was energized by knowing that there was money to be made in Lodi, Stockton, and the many other stops on the migrant trail but that the family only had a small window of opportunity—just a few days. But if she kept them working at that pace, her kids would never have to go back to Mexico. She had a vision: to see her kids established. Lupe gave all of her devotion to Juan and to her children. She never let up, and she never got sick until she was diagnosed with diabetes. But this did not slow her down, and she continued to spearhead the Soto team.

As her husband became less and less productive, Lupe remained aggressive and determined to lead the family charge. Even if Juan no longer earned as much, money would still be made if she and her kids put their backs into it. The work was heavy and dirty, but they were together as a family, and this made both Lupe and her children happy. She reminded them often that in America, the harvesting means gathering money that really grows on trees, and with money, you do not suffer. She believed it was easy money to be made and that money does grow on trees.

14. Boomtown

Eventually, the vineyards and orchards around Lodi, Stockton, and Gilroy were picked clean, so the family loaded El Tabique and ventured northward to Idaho, Washington, and Oregon. A first stop on that journey, in a western corner of Nevada, offered the family's grown-ups a rare highlight.

On the outskirts of Reno, the family overnighted in the parking lot of the Boomtown Casino. The kids were too young to enter, so they had to stay in the back of El Tabique, where they told stories and shared their dreams of the future they hoped was going to one day result from their days and nights on the migratory labor trail.

This Reno stop put them halfway to Idaho, one of the work locations they liked best. The Sierra mountains that surrounded them were beautiful. The air at the higher elevations was fresh and clean. Even though they'd each prefer a comfy bed inside the hotel, the kids loved sleeping under the thin camper shell and watching the twinkling neon casino lights beyond the camper's narrow windows. The kids took the opportunity to tailgate but watched the security guards as they risked being caught eating and sleeping in the camper.

This stop was a meaningful event for the adults, who, for one night out of the year, got a chance to play in the casino. Part of the pleasure in their gambling was imagining that they might win enough to really get ahead. But, of course, they did not score such grand winnings. Their victory was to lose the smallest amount possible, which was very little.

There was an arcade in the casino where the kids could go to have fun, but they actually preferred to stay together outside. The parents took turns checking on them. As the years went by and the kids got older, Alberto was the first to take the opportunity to go into the casino. He and Trina followed Lupe around as she circulated through the rows of flashing, chiming slot machines. She was known to have good luck against the one-armed bandits.

Trina had been an integral part of these trips since before the younger children arrived in the US. She was pitching in, alongside those children during the toughest times. Even though she once had lived like a princess in Mexico, Trina gave it her all. She wanted to make her own money so she could always pay her own way. It was a great relationship, she and Lupe living harmoniously together, both dedicated to caring for the kids.

After the family's ritual night of fun at Boomtown, early in the morning Alberto and Chayo took turns driving up north on Interstate 80 to Winnemucca, Nevada, branching north on Highway 95 to the southwestern corner of Oregon, then into western Idaho.

Idaho was the best. The family lived together in a tiny apartment there, priced at forty dollars per week. The kids dreamed of living in Idaho forever. Those were some of the happiest days of their young lives. Many of los solos whom they had met in Lodi and Stockton also showed up in Idaho. The family met other immigrants who lived in Idaho year-round. They could afford to visit their families in Mexico during the winter, so it worked out for them, except for the profound loneliness they had to endure most months of the year.

Every year, Lupe's sister Cuca, her husband Alvaro, and their two daughters Lupita and Laurie met the Soto family there. They too, followed the cherry season. They were one of the families who spent half the time in Mexico enjoying their hard-earned money. Lupe's kids always hoped that their apartment was next to Cuca's. The two girls were about between Anabel and Johnny in age, which was perfect for companionship for the kids. They also loved Cuca's delectable Betty Crocker cake dessert.

The apartments were a migrant camp known to the family as El Campo, made up of tiny apartments built out of concrete blocks. They were equipped with the basic necessities: a small stove, a refrigerator, a restroom with a tiny shower, and two small rooms. All the boys were crammed into one room filled with two bunk beds. The second room was shared between the girls and Lupe and Juan.

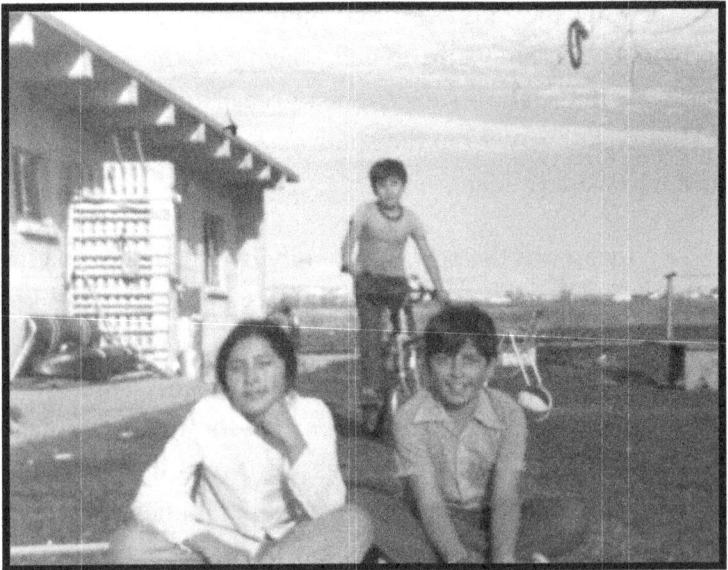

The El Campo accommodations, regardless of being tiny and lacking aesthetic appeal, were comfortable enough to beat the Lodi and Stockton labor camps, tents, and trailers.

Lupe and Juan's journey had led them here shortly after Meño was born. They had just finished the cherry season in Stockton. Betty Hernandez, the Farm Labor Contractor, notified Juan that they were moving on to Idaho, and she wanted to know if he and his wife and young boys would follow them on the picking journey there. Betty visited Lupe in the hospital and helped her fill out forms for her newborn.

Lupe brought Meño to the orchard before he was one, and when George was only a little over one year old. Lupe placed their portable crib under the cherry tree where she was going to pick, so both she and Juan could frequently check on them. Lupe had a schedule for feeding the boys and changing their diapers. Other families did the same, which made Lupe feel at ease.

It was still inconvenient to manage the kids and do her day's work too. Eventually George and Meño grew up enough to sit on a small blanket, from which they were forbidden to move. They had toys, but they preferred to play with sticks, rocks, and mud. As George got a little older, he became the babysitter. By the time they had each turned ten, they wore cherry buckets hung around their waist and picked the fruit that hung low to the ground. George did not like climbing ladders—no one did, except for Manuel, who really enjoyed it. Everything felt like a game to the kids, especially when Meño initiated some really good cherry fights. Bitten or squeezed just enough for the juice to ooze out made the best weapon. It ensured a big splatter on clothes, much like paintball stains.

Everyone wanted to pick cherries with Betty. They had the best-groomed trees and the best working equipment in the whole state. Because they knew what the life of a laborer was like, they made their orchards as desirable a place to work as possible.

Manny and Betty Hernandez were from Lindsay, and they were a shining example of what may happen in America for those who work hard for many years. One of their kids was a girl and in the same grade as Lupita. Because her parents prospered, she didn't have to skip school each year for work as Lupita had to.

The workers had to pass through a selection process to pick at Betty's orchards. The dirt parking lot filled each morning before dawn with several cars. Each carried several people wanting to work. As many as seven of los solos would emerge from one small car as if part of a circus act. Just before the sun rose, people raced across the tall, still-damp grass for ladders. The wooden ones were cold and heavy; they added extra drudgery to the workday.

However, Betty owned mostly aluminum ladders. With so many candidates desiring to be hired by her, she selected only the best pickers. Many others were turned away. Juan bristled at the wait to be selected and often opted to go somewhere else out of pride.

Whenever Juan was drunk, and until he sobered up again, the two oldest boys, Alberto and Chayo, effectively became their father's caretakers. Fueled by unresolved sorrow and loss, his displaced anger sometimes drove him to upturn the beds and paw through the furniture in search of a gun that his family had wisely hidden.

The youngest of the Soto children gradually realized, as the older ones already had, that their father was in trouble. Juan spent precious money on gambling, liquor, and beer, and many days failed to earn any money. When inebriated, he berated Lupe. She, Mama Trina, and the two girls had to hide with nearby neighbors and relatives.

Juan's attempt to quit drinking failed again and again. He entered the tiny apartment with a brown bag scrounged by his grip. The silhouette of the bag illustrated a bottle of whisky. He peeled back the paper bag, pulled out a bottle of Jack Daniels and served himself a glass; alcohol with Coca-Cola. He seemed to be in a good mood. He got to his second and third drink. He sat on a small brown old bench that he positioned propping open the apartment's rusty old door. Lupe and the girls walked in with the groceries. She greeted him with "¿Otra ves?" ("yet again?") "¡Pense que ya ibas a dejar de tragar esa porqueria!" ("I thought you were going to stop drinking that filthy thing!") If Lupe's eyes could kill, this would be the time. Juan, attempting to woo her over, looked at her and said, "Ya vente aqui sientate, vamos a platicar, las muchachas que agan la cena." ("Come here, sit down, let's talk, the girls can make dinner.") Juan instructed Anabel to get the tiny record player and play *Luces de Nueva York* ("New York Lights"), a song by La Sonora Santanera. He had Anabel or Lupita sit by the record player nervously, watching for the last note on the 7-inch single vinyl to bring the player's needle to the beginning.

During one such Idaho stay, the kids affirmed to each other that they would stand by Lupe if she divorced Juan. But that was something she would never do. She wouldn't tear her precious family apart; it would go against everything she had fought for. And although Juan was often absent due to his drinking, he always supported Lupe in her decisions and determination to keep everyone working and together.

When sober, Juan shared good advice: "Aprende a trabajar duro para no depender nunca de las ayudas del gobierno." ("Learn to work hard so that you may never rely on government aid.") "Si no puedes usar tu cerebro, usa tus manos si es necesario. Pero nunca quiero verte en la fila para cupones de alimentos o en la oficina del welfare." ("If you can't use your brain, use your hands if you must. But I never want to see you in line for food stamps or at the welfare office.")

Juan nurtured plans. He wanted to buy diesel trucks and invest in grocery stores. Even if life handed him the tragedy of his father's murder, he retained his "golden boy" upbringing, with the knowledge instilled in him about finance, life, politics, and history, as well as art, music, and literature. Perhaps these memories were part of the reason why Juan lived in torment, existing halfheartedly, equally in love with his wife and family, and with the temporary oblivion he found at the bottom of a bottle.

15. Honest Work

Once the *corrida* (run) was done in Caldwell, the Soto family started cherry picking in Emmett, Idaho, near the Payette River. A contractor there hired Juan as foreman because he had a large following of people, both families and los solos, ready to pick.

However, the orchards in this part of Idaho were on difficult slopes and lined with immensely tall trees. The twenty-two-foot ladders, called *culebritas* (snakes), were necessary in the vicinity. Sometimes they weren't tall enough to reach the most dense part of the tree. Extensions were necessary. These were usually installed by and used by los solos, usually the youngest and strongest workers.

Anabel, Prieto, Chayo and Alberto could run up and down the *culebritas* without fear. The younger children were more frightened by how these lanky contraptions swayed under their light-footed climbing. But the work still had to be done.

Next up on the migrant trail was La Grande, Oregon, nearly 150 miles from the Caldwell area. The family packed up their belongings and, upon arrival, unloaded them into giant military tents, the biggest anyone had ever seen.

La Grade was picturesque, encircled by two national parks, and filled with lush, tall green pine trees. The sun's rays peeked confidently through the heavy tree branches every morning, but the nights were freezing cold. The family's beds were thin mats laid on the ground. The hard ground and every big and little rock on it, formed an unyielding, punishing sleep environment. Every morning, the family woke up to a dewy mist inside the cold tent, with tiny water droplets coalescing on the tent's ceiling. The blankets were so cold that they seemed to be damp, even when dry.

When Lupe woke the kids up in the morning, the smell of the Folgers coffee she was drinking made the tent feel familiar and cozy. Lupita and her siblings did not drink coffee and preferred to stay under the dewy blankets, attempting to get dressed under their blankets. It was too teeth-chattering cold to get out and dress elsewhere. The boys at times, preferred to sleep under the camper shell. They walked to the picking site, carrying all the essentials for lunch, along with water and a thermos filled with coffee.

The Soto family picked cherries all day and returned to the campsite exhausted. The good thing was that several other families were camping out, so there were lots of friendly company. The boys really enjoyed the site since it was a great territory for hunting and fishing. Almost every night, the family ate fresh meat, usually venison, hunted by the boys. Once the orchard was stripped of all its fruit, the family packed up and headed back to Caldwell to resume their migrant trail.

Lupe herded the kids to the orchard before the sun filled the sky. She told them that picking fruit in the fields was good, honest work, and they should never be ashamed of it.

One never duplicated experience was picking cherries up in Wenatchee, a city in Washington State. The contractor convinced them that there was good money to be made. The Soto boys went on this expedition, not knowing what to expect. They parked El Tabique under a tree in the middle of the cherry orchard between all the trees that they had picked throughout the day. Some slept on the mattress inside the camper, two shared the truck's cabin, and the others under the truck looking for warmth. They woke up at 3:00 a.m. every day to pick until noon. The crew had about 50 workers; the majority were men. They showered to the water of the irrigation sprinklers, spraying water 100 yards. The sprinklers were in close proximity to the roads, so they had to use the cherry buckets to build a privacy wall to the passing traffic. The force of the water blew the buckets down, the men had to fill the buckets with the icy 35-degree water to keep the wall up. Ran around half naked, attempting to wash away the sorrow.

While they lived in Idaho during harvest months, the family sometimes attended the Idaho State Fair in Boise and a traditional Mexican rodeo in Caldwell. They happened to be at the rodeo near the date of Anabel's fifteenth birthday. In Mexican culture, a girl's fifteenth birthday—called a *quinceañera*—signifies that she is ready to grow into full womanhood. Parents will spend as much as they can possibly afford to make their daughter's quinceañera celebration an unforgettable moment.

During that rodeo, Hector Montemayor, a famous singer of *ranchera* tunes, performed with his band. *Rancheras* are stirring songs that celebrate the revolutionary heritage of Mexico, as well as the daily life of *la gente*, the nation's everyday people.

The Sotos listened to Montemayor's best-loved songs, including "Barrio Pobre*"* ("Poor Town") and "Consejos de un Padre" ("Advice from a Father"). After the performance, Juan managed to get backstage. There, he asked the famous singer and his mariachi band to come play at the Soto family's small apartment so Anabel could have a splendid quinceañera.

Everyone around the labor camp gathered to enjoy the performance, praising and thanking Juan for providing this treat. Juan enjoyed feeling his "golden boy" heritage again. His bruised soul took in nourishment on that day. Despite the family's fall from the astounding wealth it possessed in the past to scrabbling for a living in a once-foreign land, on this very significant day, Juan Soto was able to emulate the generosity of spirit for which his father, Rosario Soto, was so well known.

16. Apple Harvest

The migrant labor experience was all about making the most of your precious resources. Economists might call it "maximizing utility."

For Lupe and Juan's family, the strategy was to keep their crew of themselves and their children able to keep on earning, every day that their human limitations would allow. So, when the Sotos weren't eating or sleeping, they were filling their days with work. As the weeks and months of harvest season went by, the kind of work and where to find it, were in constant flux.

Summer's hottest days were spent working onion fields in Oregon, Washington, and Idaho. There was no shade for humans, just a little for the bugs who lived at ground level. The bugs walked and stood as they pleased, but the people had to work while stooped over. It was like being an athlete, but the only glory was the fact that you were feeding yourself and the people you love with the *poco dinero* (little money) you're making.

Like leeks and garlic, onions grow flowering tops that produce the seed stock for next year's crop. But most of the tops get cut off, so the plants will grow larger. So the first round of labor was *la mota* "topping" the onions. Soon, it was *la espiga* pulling out the tassel from the top of corn stalks. To encourage the kids through those hot, muggy summer days, Juan would promise the kids all earnings working the la mota, espiga, and onions were theirs to keep.

When the onions had all been tended to, the family's next place of work would be in a corn cannery. Canneries offered shade beneath a corrugated tin or aluminum roof but also had steam from the massive cooking kettles and clangorous noise from the production line. Safety was an issue, too, with conveyor belts that could trap and perhaps maim or sever fingers, hands, or arms. That production line was seldom halted, since owners of the cannery maximized utility by keeping the line moving at the fastest possible pace. Empty cans rattled into place to be filled with corn kernels, then, further down the line, their lids were soldered on. Eventually, the cans were stuffed into cases that would ride in big trucks to warehouses.

Nyssa, Oregon, sat alongside the Snake River in the eastern-central section of the state, close to the Idaho border and the town of Caldwell, where the Sotos once spent a year. The corn cannery in Nyssa was called American Fine Foods, and that was where the family worked for a month or two every year, starting in mid-August.

Primo knew the owners and built a very good relationship with them. They loved him, and they also loved the burritos that Lupe often brought them for lunch. The Soto kids were able to work at the cannery as soon as they turned fifteen and could handle the easier jobs. Lupe ran the conveyor belts. They were controlled by a panel of buttons that stopped the belts at her touch. The other cannery ladies whispered to each other, wondering how Lupe got that "easy job" even though her English-speaking ability was limited. But Lupe did not have to speak the language to understand how a business works and how the conveyor system worked; she was loyal and hard working.

The kids appreciated working in the corn cannery. They got out of the hot and dirty fields and could dress casually in American-made jeans and a regular shirt or blouse. They could stay a little cleaner, though some jobs required wearing plastic aprons. Anabel and Lupita enjoyed getting dolled up with makeup and lipstick just like the other teenage girls at the cannery. However, the work was tiring, very repetitive, lasted from eight to twelve hours a day, and often required more hours of work on weekends. Anabel started there at fourteen, running a machine that sealed the cans. Lupita sorted the corn on the conveyor belt, by far one of the toughest jobs inside the cannery. The boys worked in shipping, receiving, driving forklifts, loading trucks, and doing paperwork.

The drive home was rather long from Nyssa, which bordered Idaho. The family drove 95 to Parma, Idaho. It was customary to stop at a local liquor store in Parma. Juan parked across the 95 and the family ran across the road as soon as it was safe. That stop was one of the highlights of the day, because the children had their choice of snack, along with a super cold, refreshing, bubbly Coca-Cola or chocolate-covered vanilla ice cream, or perhaps both, depending on the temperature outside and Juan's mood. The kids picked their favorite snack, and Juan picked a bottle of whiskey. Then they loaded up in the camper in the back of El Tabique and drove down 95 to 20 into Caldwell, Idaho.

September brought the onset of autumn, and also the toughest work of the entire year: harvesting apples. To make the most of their opportunity, after Idaho, the family packed up and drove to the Wenatchee Valley, "The Apple Capital of the World," in central Washington where the Columbia and Wenatchee Rivers unite as they then flow south, and where apples have been commercially grown for nearly a hundred years.

Apple picking commenced at sunrise. The whole family worked all day long in their cold, soaking wet socks and shoes. They wore cotton gloves for warmth and not to bruise the apples. But those gloves were soon wet, too, and would stay so continuously. Fingers were soon numb with cold. Warming the gloves and feet became a ritual whenever the sun poked through the clouds.

The heavy fruit got picked into heavy sacks made of canvas and tin, built so they expanded as they got filled up. The pickers had to carry loaded bags from the trees to dump into large wooden bins throughout the day.

It was relentless work from sunup until right before dusk: lift a heavy ladder, climb, pick, dismount, fill the bin, then repeat, steadily, all day long. Everyone got exhausted.

Lupe fed her family superb burritos for their apple-orchard lunches. Out of necessity, they were served cold. But Lupe's tortilla-wrapped creations might have inspired gourmets to travel for miles. The entire crew sought out her cooking, even when it was only ham and cheese sandwiches and hard-boiled eggs, with a side of Doritos.

Some people on the picking crews knew about Juan's drinking, but still, he sustained a great reputation with them, as well as with the ranch and orchard owners and the labor contractors. His family displayed such a strong work ethic and exemplary personal values. They were a handsome and determined group, and people gave Juan a lot of credit.

111

In fact, Juan was often named field supervisor or foreman. He succeeded by character and charisma, the same as his late father did. And so, Lupe made extra burritos for him to give to field owners, field managers, and the other workers. Like Rosario Soto, Juan provided a welcome bit of largesse, customary in Mexican culture, befitting his status.

At the end of the apple harvest each year, the family drove back home to Lindsay, a journey of nearly nine hundred miles.

17. Always about the Kids

Life as migrant laborers was both sweet and bitter.

It was sweet because the entire Soto family was now back together again, with old and new family members in the mix, succeeding as they created new lives thousands of miles away from the scene of their grandfather's murder. They were learning a new language, discovering delectable new foods, experiencing intriguing new things, and were kept together by Lupe's unconquerable spirit—with abundant help from Mama Trina—and by the values both women imparted through their actions.

It was bitter, too, for many reasons. Silent hostility often radiated from the eyes of strangers, turning happy moments into guarded ones. Many of the family's nights together had to be spent in a cold tent above rocky ground in the Sierra Nevada foothills, with everyone aware that the exhausting daily work would begin again at dawn.

Juan and Lupe remained vigilant and protective of their children, even when they became fully grown. This was especially true regarding Lupita and Anabel, who now realized that their parents were just as strict with teenage girls as their grandparents had been a generation earlier in Michoacán.

Slowly, the Soto team got smaller and smaller. Kids graduated and took on other jobs or went to college.

Alberto, the oldest child, was the first one to graduate from high school. The family was too young to understand that piece of American culture, with its rituals like graduation. When Alberto graduated from high school in June 1979, the family was already picking cherries in Idaho. Juan and Lupe knew that he had to stay behind and finish out the year in order to complete high school. He stayed home in Lindsay to finish the school year as required, then decided to participate in the graduation ceremony. There is a picture of Alberto in his cap and gown alone in Lindsay High School, and despite the fact that he actually had a big, loving family, none of them attended. The trade-offs were sometimes high and harder than the family hoped. Alberto was one of the smartest kids in the family, not just because he was the oldest, but because he had a good head on his shoulders and used it wisely. He led the way in high school education and graduations. The environment for a migrant student in high school America seemed tough—you have cultural differences, peer pressure from friends, classmates, teachers, in addition to trying to fit in. For Alberto, it also meant learning the English language quickly to be able to keep up with all of it and still earn enough credits to graduate and receive his diploma, which was a great accomplishment.

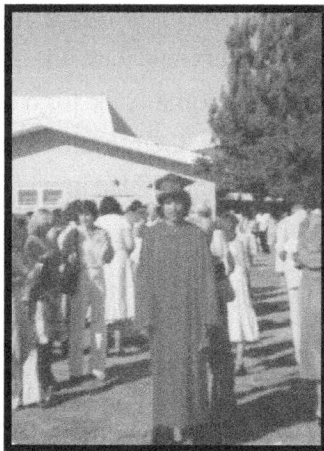

Alberto quickly realized that many things that might have come to him easily in Mexico now had to be attained the hard way. Alberto wanted to continue his education and still had dreams of becoming a doctor, but he had to choose between his aspirations, which came with many barriers, and helping Lupe and Juan bring in money to support the family. Lacking citizenship, he could not legally aspire to attend college. He decided to continue picking fruits and vegetables in the fields alongside Lupe and Juan. After high school, he studied to become a diesel mechanic. At the same time, he learned to play the electric bass and joined with other local boys to form a band called Super Tropical Universo with songs such as La Guayaba, La Cumbia De Los Pajaritos and Mentira. Alberto was a mainstay of their work treks for his first years in California, but he could earn even more money by playing music at parties and gatherings with his band. Music paid enough to get him excused from the migrant trail, so he remained in Lindsay and took responsibility for meeting the mortgage payments on the Fresno Street house while the rest of the family followed the harvests.

Chayo wanted to enroll in the navy or Air Force. He went to an Air Force recruiting office to enroll. He was scheduled for his first interview with the recruiter, all went well, and he was asked to come back for a second interview. During the second interview, the recruiter asked him, "Where do you see yourself in ten years?" He looked around the room and saw a picture of a US fighter jet hanging on the wall. Chayo pointed at the photo and said to the recruiter, "Flying one of those fighter jets." The recruiter responded, "I'm going to be honest with you. You are not going to be able to fly one of those because you are a first generation citizen of the US, and only people of the fifth generation can fly those fighter jets." Whether true or not, Chayo could not verify that information at that time—he trusted what the recruiter said and because of that response, Chayo decided not to enlist.

Chayo eventually earned a GED via continuation classes. His grades were strong enough to allow him to enter Cal Poly, at the San Luis Obispo campus.

When Anabel started high school, she got to walk forty-five minutes each way from home with a neighbor because Chayo and Alberto worked early in the morning picking oranges and lemons. In the school year 1980–81, Anabel did not attend high school because Juan did not want Anabel attending school by herself without Alberto and Chayo. Alberto had already graduated, Chayo was off to continuation school, and Primo was in junior high school. Juan was extremely strict with the girls; Anabel was not allowed to attend high school by herself. When Primo entered high school, Anabel resumed classes.

During the week of her graduation, Anabel became sick with an unexplainable pain in her stomach. Lupe gave her home remedies as she did back in Mexico. She had no medical insurance. So she gave her olive oil, castor oil, a mixture of lemon and Arm & Hammer baking soda, Cola de Caballo tea, and Yerba Buena tea. Nothing was working, and Anabel held on to her stomach as she hobbled over in pain. She was rushed to the hospital. The diagnosis was appendicitis, and they removed her appendix during surgery. The doctor instructed her not to walk or wear high heels for her graduation, and directed her to wear slippers. The day of her graduation, the principal called out each student by name and each student took their turn walking across the Lindsay high school auditorium. Kids jumped up, cheered, and shook hands as

116

they walked past their schoolmates to receive their diplomas. The proud parents and families in the audience clapped and took photos. When Anabel's name was announced over the loudspeaker, we all expected her to stand and then sit, with no walking as the doctor ordered. Instead, Anabel got up in heels and walked slowly, at a snail's pace, up to the front and crossed the auditorium just like everyone else. People clapped and cheered. She was still walking after the cheering stopped. She stopped for a second and then continued at an even slower pace. The crowd got up and cheered some more. A fellow student got up and helped her walk across the auditorium to receive her diploma. She had not come this far just to let a little ol' appendicitis stop her from participating in the American ritual of high school graduation.

Juan and Lupe discovered that high school graduation is a form of rite of passage in the US and learned that High School was equivalent to *La Preparatoria* in Mexico's school system. After Knowing this and understanding that the Soto kids mastered the academic skills and completed the high school's graduation credits requirements required by American standards, and they did it in English, their second language, Juan and Lupe were proud of each one. After Anabel's graduation, all the kids after her had huge celebrations. Chayo did not graduate from high school but did receive his GED, later graduated from the Police Academy. Chayo by far, had the biggest cheering section on the stands. Juan did not attend but was very proud, so proud that this was one of the reasons he stopped drinking. So, every year the entire family attended graduations and still managed to make it to the cherries.

18. Family

For the Soto family, a vacation came in the form of a visit to Tia Teresa's house in Salinas. She and her family owned several El Charito markets in the area, with the main store on Market Street. This was where the family gathered because there was a deli with the best chile verde burritos, homemade tortillas, and churros (donut-like pastries made in a straight line instead of a circle). A line formed out the door and around the building daily. It was the only type of road trip that did not involve picking some type of fruit or vegetable.

The kids jumped into a plush, comfortable taffeta van that Juan owned for a short while. Juan drove with Lupe as the passenger, Trina and Anabel at the captain's chairs, the rest of the kids competed for the seat in the back and space on the floor. Driving North on 99 was quiet for the family as anticipation grew in their bellies. It wasn't until they passed the tunnel of giant oak trees precisely after San Juan Bautista as you hop on 101 South towards Salinas that the kids started cheering. Seeing the wall of giant oak trees along the side of the road was a sure sign that they were headed to Salinas, not Stockton or Lodi, and this made the kids happy.

The Mountains fell behind them as their scenery changed to open land filled with strawberry fields. The atmosphere was different, the air was crisp with a hint of ocean, the temperature a bit chilly, and a sense of freedom was felt throughout their bodies. Salinas was different from Lindsay. To them, it was a big city with streets filled with busy, well-groomed people going into work in the beautifully lit buildings in the city's downtown area.

The three-hour drive was an exciting and happy occasion for Lupe and her kids. It meant they were visiting with Lupe's sisters and her mom, their grandmother. Tia Teresa's home was beautiful and perfect, it was in the Hartnell Community College area. They had things the kids had only dreamed of or seen on *The Brady Bunch*. Tia Teresa's home was clean, modern, and elegant with a grand piano at the entrance.

One particular trip during Easter break in 1984, Lupe and Juan agreed to allow Anabel and Lupita to stay behind in Salinas the entire week to work at the store and earn a few dollars.

But instead of being made to work, the girls were treated like true family and spent their time enjoying Tia Teresa's company.

That summer, after cherry picking ended in Stockton and Lodi, some members of the Soto family went off to Salinas instead of Idaho. Juan and Lupe rented a two-bedroom apartment. Juan had intentions of buying a small grocery store in Salinas or a nearby city. Teresa offered employment to Anabel and Primo. Juan and Lupe found work at a local flower distribution center where Juana, another of Lupe's sisters, worked. When August 1984 came around, Primo, along with Lupita, Johnny, George, and Meño, enrolled in Salinas schools.

One month into that school year, Anabel eloped. Lupe was devastated. She blamed Teresa, accusing her of supporting and aiding the elopement. Lupe desperately called everyone she could think of in the small kitchen of the Salinas apartment, hoping to reach Anabel and talk sense into her. She wanted her daughter back. But as the night sky got inky black and the little kitchen became dark, Lupe realized that Anabel was not coming back. Her anger turned to pain. The tears started falling and would not stop. She cried in pain, the strong woman who led her family through years of migrant work all across California and the Pacific Northwest looked defeated. Still seeking an explanation, she wanted more than anything to see Anabel walk through the apartment door.

The family immediately returned to Lindsay, minus Anabel.

Lupe cried for days. "Nadie entiende realmente el dolor de una madre y el amor por sus hijos hasta que se convierten en madre," she insisted over and over again. ("No one really understands the pain of a mother and the love for her children until they become a mother.") Lupe felt betrayed, she would not speak to her sister and her family for many years to come.

The year 1988 was the last year for Lupe and Juan along with Johnny, George, and Meño to drive the migrant trail. The rest of the Soto clan had started new lives with school or jobs, but they still had many difficult passages ahead.

Johnny, their little Juanito, reached his twenty-seven year only to fall victim one night on the streets of nearby Fresno to a drunk driver who was recklessly trying to outrace police pursuit.

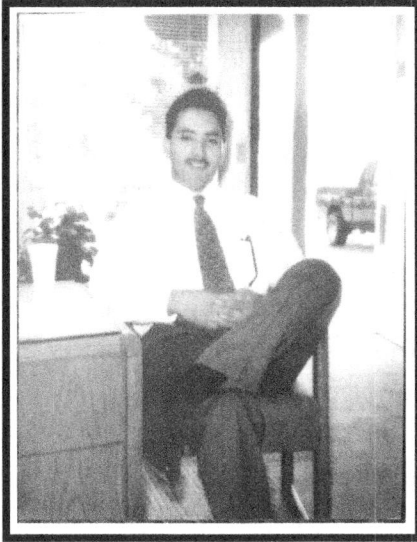

This event shook the family to its core. At first, the family only knew that Juanito was in an accident in Fresno. They spent the entire night calling hospitals looking for him, and getting no word. Finally, Juanito's girlfriend called Lupe with the bad news. She fell to pieces. In her extreme grief, she wrongly felt to blame for her son's death. Only a week before, Lupe had discarded a bothersome chain letter. It had predicted a nameless tragedy would strike unless she sent it on to ten more people. She had bouts of uncontrollable crying and fainted off and on. Her children watched her, unsure how to help her with such sorrow and pain. But Juan took her arms and said, "Esto no es tu culpa. Componte y piense en tu salud y en la de tus hijos y nietos. Ellos te necesitan. No hay nada que podamos hacer para cambiar las circunstancias." ("This is not your fault. Compose yourself. Think about your health and the kids and grandkids. They need you. There is nothing we can do to change the circumstances.") A second later, he added, "ni modo" ("no way") for emphasis. Lupe sat on the bed as he consoled her.

Once she was comforted, Juan calmly gave his children assignments. Alberto, Chayo, Anabel, and Lupita were to coordinate the funeral arrangements, including the church, funeral home, and flowers. He made one request, that Juanito's casket should be white. He said, "El ataúd de Juanito tiene que ser blanco. El nunca entró en la santidad del matrimonio, por esa razón su ataúd debe ser blanco." ("Juanito's coffin has to be white. He never entered into the sanctity of marriage, for that reason, his coffin must be white.") Then Juan walked straight out of their bedroom through the hallway and straight out the front door, without a word to anyone else. He got in his truck with a heavy heart and defeat in his face and drove away.

Despite being an open field, the perfumed graveyard was filled with a sea of mourners, making it difficult to maneuver through the crowd that showed up to say their goodbyes to Johnny. No dry eye in sight from old to young; family, friends, and Juan's pickers gathered around his heavenly white casket. The family felt the support and love from all who were present. A mariachi band walked at a hazy distance, and as they got to a hearing distance, began to play "La Media Vuelta" by Luis Miguel (a famous Mexican pop star), followed by "Cruz de Olvido," typically sang by Vicente Fernandez. The mariachi continued as the people approached and paid their respects to the Soto family. Juanito,

"Johnny," wanted it that way—"Celebrate life and leave no room for tears," he'd say.

Juan had just quit drinking several months prior. The entire family and close relatives were concerned that he was going to hit the bottle again. But he never touched it again.

The calamity did not break the Soto family's spirit. Remarkably, Juan—a problem drinker who had lost both a doting father and a beloved son to senseless violence—deserved much of the credit for his family's resilience. He found ways to keep the family together and strong, moving forward. He remained sober and strong. He guided the children and provided advice, communicating and keeping the family together and moving forward positively, reassuring them to keep pushing to stay on a straight path. He affirmed many times, "Mantente comprometida, humilde y honesta." ("Stay committed, humble, and honest.")

Old age befell Mama Trina, who became wheelchair-bound by kidney disease, which quickly took her life. Lupe, after ten years of faithfully taking care of Mama Trina, had to watch as her mother-in-law passed away. Trina had once been such a beautiful young girl that the richest man for many miles around had ordered her kidnapped, hoping she would become his bride. Lupe was never quite the same after the loss of her great friend who nurtured her children for so many years.

In time, though, all of Juan and Lupe's surviving kids tasted success, thanks to the striving ways their mother had taught them. Juan bought his first diesel truck to start a family business and named it Soto Trucking. He wanted his kids to stop working in the fields. Alberto and Chayo received their commercial driver's licenses and joined the family business, where they both started as the company drivers and eventually hired other truck drivers. Chayo became the first of the eight siblings to marry and the first to become a father. His first daughter, Suzette, was born in 1984. She was the first of many beautiful first experiences for the family. She was the first granddaughter, the first baby, the first niece, the first baby girl, and had the first real quinceañera. Juan and Lupe were delighted to have her. Juan said she brought so much joy and happiness into their world.

Everyone was looking forward to having the entire family together. Kids practiced tirelessly for weeks the choreographed traditional waltz dance (El Valce) to be performed during the awaited quinceañera. All together her fourteen Damas and their partners made up the quinceañera's court. The celebration, similar to a bat mitzvah, is a girl's fifteenth birthday and her transition from childhood to adulthood. The celebration included a traditional mass with the offering of a bouquet of flowers to the Virgin Mary followed by a party. Chayo and Cindy, invited four hundred guests. The party was held at Tulare Memorial in Tulare, a town about ten minutes west of Lindsay. The dense fog in January did not keep people away; five hundred people from all over California, Idaho, Oregon, and Mexico arrived in their fancy cars, typically stored in the garage waiting for a special occasion. Men in three-piece suits, cufflinks, shiny shoes, Women in lavish cocktail dresses, brand name shoes and handbags. Family, friends, police officers, and Juan's pickers joined in the celebration—many uninvited guests were turned away because they had reached the building's capacity. The hall came alive with a DJ and a mariachi that circled the hall for three hours (most parties hire for one hour). Mariachi music has a way of bringing people together. The Soto family offered the guests an open bar, bountiful food, laughter, joy, and happiness-energy dressed the walls of Tulare Memorial as family and friends danced like it was 1999 (it was 1999). A memory in time worth the $28,000 spent by the family. Juan, extremely proud, sober grandfather, stayed until the last guest left the building.

Alberto and Chayo kept the family business prospering for many years to come by becoming agricultural contractors. They ventured in citrus, cherries, and olive business, signing up to 430 payroll checks per week. Chayo trained in police work and retired after seventeen years of service.

Anabel started a successful bridal boutique, Annabelle's Bridal Boutique, in Visalia. Anabel was widowed with three kids at a young age when she was left to start from ground up to build a successful business. She is a civic minded individual and community steward. She served one year as President of Rotary International and President of Tulare/Kings County Hispanic Chamber of Commerce for several years. Anabel has been nominated for the Tulare County and Kings County Chamber of Commerce Woman of the year amongst many other nominations and award recipient. She has served as a board member to Pan America Bank, Downton Visalians, Foundations of Tulare and Kings County and National Latino Peace Officers Association. Primo had a prosperous career with Costco Wholesale who successfully opened 7-8 Warehouse stores throughout the country. He runs his own thriving housing development and construction business. George became Plant Manager of a large citrus company with acreage throughout the San Joaquin Valley and the Sierra Nevada foothills. He leads a group of up to 180 people and is highly respected within his industry.

Lupita was the first female in her family to earn a college degree (Johnny was the first in the family to earn a college degree), which led to a human resources career in Silicon Valley.

Before passing, Johnny had a passion for education, he wanted to be the first one from the family to attend and graduate from college. He wanted to lead the way, break the invisible barriers, and set a good example for the next generation to come. He enrolled in California State University Fresno where he studied Agriculture and received Agricultural Business degree. He was the first male in the family to graduate from a university.

Lupe worked and lived for her children. Everything she did, including all the early mornings, long days, sacrifices, sleeping under freezing cold tents, and everything she gave up was all done for her kids.

19. Don Juan

Juan remained a handsome man, remarkably fit-looking as he entered his sixties. But his belly now displayed an almost feminine roundness. His liver was silently ballooning. In time, it would fail. This was a side effect of the cirrhosis that decades of hard drinking had brought on.

For years, Juan knew that he had blood poisoning as a result of worsening kidney failure, but he refused treatment. "Once you check into a hospital," he reasoned to the family, "you don't get out alive."

In 1990, Lupe was at a doctor's visit. She asked her doctor if he would also see Juan. The doctor tested his blood sugar level, and all looked normal. But then a blood test revealed diabetes, complicating the kidney failure. The doctor placed Juan on a strict diet. However, the patient refused to follow his doctor's orders. Juan wanted a second opinion and sought medical treatment while visiting the house in La Piedad. Juanito and George were with him for support. The La Piedad doctor gave him medication to treat his diabetes. Juan then returned to the US but still refused treatment for kidney failure.

His body could take no more. Juan was placed in a hospital, the exact place he had feared to go. His grown children gathered around his hospital bed. They saw hope in Juan's eyes, mixed with a look that said, "I'm sorry." He spent a month in the hospital, optimistically planning his dialysis days.

Juan's children and grandchildren visited frequently, making sure he was well taken care of in the hospital, conversing with doctors, looking for solutions and best care possible. Lupe never left his side.

However, the blood poisoning didn't yield to treatment. Gangrene infected both of his legs, the same once-powerful legs that had carried him up and down the *culebrita* ladders and throughout vineyards, ranches, and orchards in most of the western states. Juan's final hours were spent on a morphine drip. But in his better days, he had been the family's nucleus of respect, a source of strength and confidence.

El Tabique's pilot was gone, but his remaining family had collectively built a foundation for their future. This foundation was exactly why Lupe had always rejected the idea of divorcing him, even in the scariest and darkest parts of their marriage, and even when her children said they would understand and support such a decision. Lupe maintained that divorce would not have been good for her children's futures.

With Juan's passing, the Soto family dynamic shifted. The grown children became busier as they established their own lives, identities, and young families. They did not show up quite as automatically for each holiday and family event. Even Thanksgiving and Christmas felt quite different. The familial connectedness was still deeply felt but was no longer the dominant force in all of the grown-up Soto kids' lives.

Then, in February 2018, Meño, the youngest of the Sotos and a Californian by birth, suddenly passed in his sleep one night. This shook Lupe, and she began to question her decisions throughout her life. Meño was her baby boy. She second-guessed herself, "¿Tomé la decisión correcta de perseguir a Juan a América? ("did I make the right decision to chase Juan to America?") "Si tan solo me hubiera quedado en México, mis hijos Juanito y Meño estarían vivos." ("If only I had stayed in Mexico, my kids, Juanito and Meño would still be alive.") Her health turned for the worst, and she lost unhealthy weight and cried uncontrollably. Juan, her rock, her golden boy was not alive to comfort her to tell her everything will be alright. She found peace in God.

In 2020 and well into 2021, the COVID-19 pandemic sadly all but obliterated the family's patterns of contact. Family events had always been the happiest times they had ever known, even during the hardships of immigrant labor and the constant need to keep moving and keep working.

Like Juan Soto, who lost his father yet never learned to grieve, Lupe's adult children struggled to achieve acceptance of the changes that time delivered to them. Lupe's unyielding faith in God kept her strong when she needed to be strong. She is grateful and proud of her children, twenty-two grandkids, and fourteen great--grandkids. She says, "Aunque

133

no completos, falta el principal: Juan, el líder de la familia de fuerza, ha dejado un gran vacío en la familia, pero ay que seguir adelante y asi, el era muy orgulloso de su familia." ("Although not complete, the main one is missing: Juan, the leader of the family of strength, has left a great void in the family, but we must move on and as such, he was very proud of his family.")

To this day, Lupe encounters people who knew her husband. They speak fondly of his memory. When the next-door neighbors moved in early 2021, the man told Lupe that he had once worked for Juan and had nothing but respect and admiration for him. He gave Juan Soto the honorable title "Don Juan," as many did when he was alive and still do now.

Juan Soto left a legacy that many admire; his reputation and core values were undeniable and people from all over sought him out for advice and support, financial and professional. He'd allow people to live in the casita or the room in the back – many times for free. His strong character and core values precede him. So many individuals recognize such legacy he influenced from Mexico, California, Idaho, Washington Montana to Nevada.

Lupe remains the center of the family's identity, though many of her children have dispersed to other parts of California, some even away from the Golden State in which each began the demanding processes of adapting to and embracing the culture of the United States of America.

Lupe's still a great cook. She happily busies herself in her kitchen on those occasions when family, friends, and neighbors drop by. She still walks into downtown Lindsay every morning, anonymous to most of those who see her— just an older Mexican-American lady.

Most who see her don't realize it, but a spirit so brave as hers is rare, and indescribably beautiful.

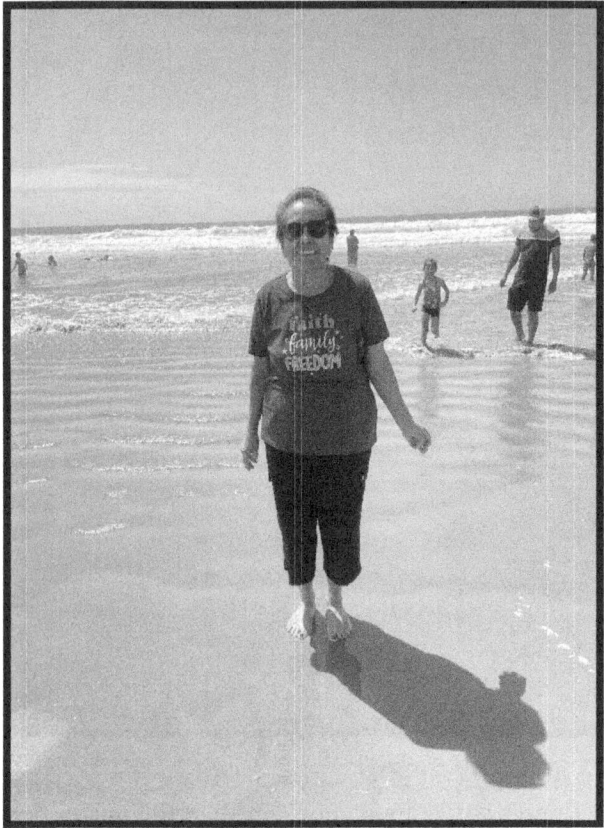

Made in the USA
Las Vegas, NV
09 January 2024